RIBBONS, MEDALS AND REGIMENTAL BADGES

PART I.—RIBBONS AND MEDALS

PART II.—REGIMENTS AT A GLANCE

The Naval & Military Press Ltd

Published by

The Naval & Military Press Ltd

Unit 10 Ridgewood Industrial Park,
Uckfield, East Sussex,
TN22 5QE England

Tel: +44 (0) 1825 749494
Fax: +44 (0) 1825 765701

www.naval-military-press.com
www.military-genealogy.com

PREFACE.

THIS small volume, started early in 1915, does not pretend to give a full, authoritative, or complete account of all the Orders, Decorations, and Medals which have ever been bestowed upon British subjects. Neither is it intended for the expert collector. It aims principally at providing a means whereby the ordinary person may recognise the ribbon of any Order or Medal he sees on the breast of a British soldier or sailor, and for this purpose actual pieces of the different ribbons have been reproduced.

To keep the book within reasonable limits, foreign Orders and Decorations, save in a few exceptional cases, have been excluded.

My thanks are due to Mr. D. Hastings Irwin, for permission to make use of information in his valuable book "War Medals and Decorations," and to Mr. A. H. Baldwin, of Duncannon Street, London, W.C., who has assisted me to collect the necessary ribbons for reproduction, and has given me many valuable hints. Also to Mr. E. Emanuel, of Portsmouth, for his help, and to the Secretaries of the Royal Humane Society, the Royal National Life-boat Institution, and the Society for Protection of Life from Fire, for details of the medals awarded by these bodies.

I should be grateful if any suggestions or mistakes could be notified to me c/o the Publishers.

TAPRELL DORLING,
Lieutenant-Commander,
Royal Navy.

CONTENTS

ONE HUNDRED AND TWENTY-EIGHT
RIBBONS
NAVAL, MILITARY AND CIVIL

ONE HUNDRED AND TWENTY-EIGHT RIBBONS
NAVAL, MILITARY AND CIVIL

NOTE.—The Number of each Ribbon corresponds with the Number in the Descriptive Letterpress, pages 13–75.

3. Order of the Bath.

6. Order of St. Michael and St George.

10. Imperial Service Order and Medal.

2. Victoria Cross, Army.

5. Order of the Star of India

9. Distinguished Service Order

8. Royal Victorian Order.

1. Victoria Cross, Navy.

4. Order of Merit.

7. Order of the Indian Empire.

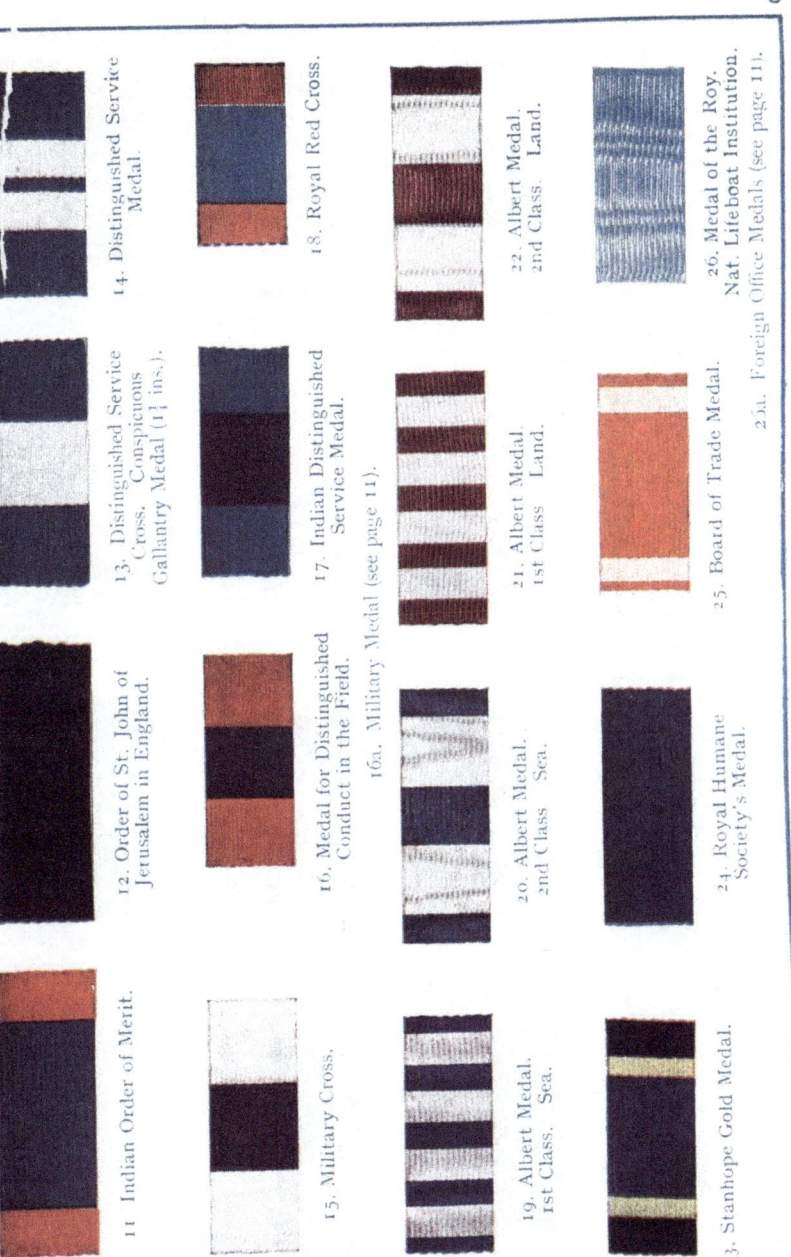

3

11. Indian Order of Merit.

12. Order of St. John of Jerusalem in England.

13. Distinguished Service Cross. Conspicuous Gallantry Medal (1¼ ins.).

14. Distinguished Service Medal.

15. Military Cross.

16. Medal for Distinguished Conduct in the Field.

16a. Military Medal (see page 11).

17. Indian Distinguished Service Medal.

18. Royal Red Cross.

19. Albert Medal. 1st Class. Sea.

20. Albert Medal. 2nd Class. Sea.

21. Albert Medal. 1st Class. Land.

22. Albert Medal. 2nd Class. Land.

23. Stanhope Gold Medal.

24. Royal Humane Society's Medal.

25. Board of Trade Medal.

26. Medal of the Roy. Nat. Lifeboat Institution.

26a. Foreign Office Medals (see page 11).

4

ONE HUNDRED AND TWENTY-EIGHT RIBBONS
NAVAL, MILITARY AND CIVIL

NOTE.—The Number of each Ribbon corresponds with the Number in the Descriptive Letterpress, pages 13–75.

27 Edward Medal.

28 King's Police Medal. (See footnote p. 38.)

29 Medal of the Society for the Protection of Life from Fire.

30 Jubilee and Diamond Jubilee Medals, 1887 and 1897.

31 Police Medals, Jubilee and Diamond Jubilee, 1887 and 1897.

32 Coronation Medal, 1902.

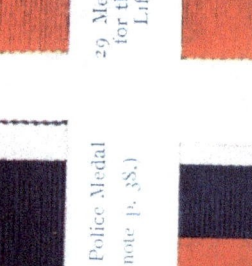
33 Police Coronation Medal, 1902.

34 Durbar Medal, 1903.

35 King Edward's Medal, Ireland, 1903.

36 King George's Coronation and Durbar Medals

37 King George's Police Coronation Medal

38 King's Visit Commemoration Medal, Ireland, 1911.

5

39. Union of South Africa Commemoration Medal.

40. Kaisar-i-Hind Medal.

41. Badge of the Order of the League of Mercy.

42. St. John of Jerusalem Service Medal.

43. St. John of Jerusalem, South Africa, 1899–1902.

44. Arctic and Antarctic.

45. Best Shot in the British Army.

46. Naval Good Shooting Medal.

47. Transport Medal

48. Naval General Service Medal, 1793–1840.

49. Military Gen. Service, 1793–1814. Waterloo, 1815. Burmah, 1824–26.

50. India Medal, 1799–1826.

51. Capture of Ghuznee, July, 1839.

52. Jellalabad, 1842. 1842–43 India Medals. Kabul–Kandahar, 1880.

53. China, 1842.

54. Sutlej Campaign (Sikh War), 1845–46.

6

ONE HUNDRED AND TWENTY-EIGHT RIBBONS NAVAL, MILITARY AND CIVIL

NOTE.—The Number of each Ribbon corresponds with the Number in the Descriptive Letterpress, pages 13–75.

55. New Zealand, 1855–66.

56. Punjab, 1848–49.

57. India General Service, 1854

58. South Africa, 1834–35, 1846–47, 1850–53, 1877–79.

59. Crimea, 1854–56.

60. Baltic, 1854–55.

61. Indian Mutiny, 1857–58.

62. First Design for China Ribbon.

63. China 1857–60.

64. Canada General Service, 1866–70.

65. Abyssinia, 1867–68.

66. Ashantee, 1873–74. East and West Africa, 1887–1900.

7

67. Afghanistan, 1878-80.

68. Cape of Good Hope, 1880-97.

69. Egypt, 1882-89.

70. North-West Canada, 1885.

71. Matabeleland, 1893.
Rhodesia, 1896.
Mashonaland, 1897.

72. Ashanti Star

73. India Medal, 1895.

74. Central Africa, 1891-98.

75. Soudan, 1896-97

76. East and Central Africa, 1897-99.

77. Royal Niger Company, 1886-97.

78. South Africa, Queen Victoria's, 1899-1902.

79. South Africa, King Edward's, 1901-02

80. China, 1900.

81. Ashanti, 1901.

82. Africa General Service, 1902.

ONE HUNDRED AND TWENTY-EIGHT RIBBONS NAVAL, MILITARY AND CIVIL

NOTE.—The Number of each Ribbon corresponds with the Number in the Descriptive Letterpress, pages 13-75.

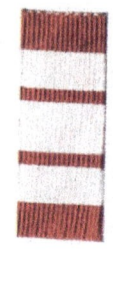

86. Naval General Service, 1915.

85. India General Service, 1908

84. Tibet, 1903-04.

83. Zulu Rising, Natal, 1906.

90. Vol. and Reserve Officers' Decorations (1½ ins.). Vol. L.S., etc. (1¼ ins.)

89. Meritorious Service, Royal Marines

88. Long Service and Good Conduct—Army. (See also 26a, page 11.)

87. Long Service and Good Conduct—Navy

94. Special Reserve Long Service and Good Conduct.

93. Militia Long Service and Good Conduct.

92. Imperial Yeomanry Long Service and Good Conduct

91. Territorial Decoration (1½ ins.). Territorial Efficiency Medal (1¼ ins.).

9

95. Cape of Good Hope. Long Service and Good Conduct

96. Tasmania. Long Service and Good Conduct

98. Australian Commonwealth. Long Service and Good Conduct.

97. West African Frontier Force. Long Service and Good Conduct

99. New South Wales. Long Service and Good Conduct.

100. Queensland. Long Service and Good Conduct.

101. Natal. Long Service and Good Conduct

102. Permanent Overseas Forces. Long Service and Good Conduct.

103. West Africa Troops Distinguished Conduct Medal.

104. Australian Commonwealth—Meritorious Service.

105. Turkish Medal for Crimea.

106. Sardinian Medal for Crimea.

107. Medal for Chitral Maharajah of Jummoo and Kashmir

108. Bronze Star, 1882–9⋅

109. Khedive's Sudan Medal 1896–1905.

110. Sudan Medal, 1910–12.

ONE HUNDRED AND TWENTY-EIGHT RIBBONS NAVAL, MILITARY AND CIVIL

NOTE.—The Number of each Ribbon corresponds with the Number in the Descriptive Letterpress, pages 13–75.

114. Croix de Guerre (France).

113. Medaille Militaire (France).

112. Legion of Honour (France).

111. Messina Medal (Italy).

117. Order of Leopold (Belgium).

116. Order of St George (Russia).

115. Order of St. Stanislas (Russia).

120. Order of the Golden Kite (Japan).

119. Order of the Sacred Treasure (Japan).

118. Order of the Rising Sun (Japan).

11

121. Iron Cross (Prussia),
Military.

122. Iron Cross (Prussia),
Civil

123. Order of the Medjidie
(Turkey).

124. Order of the Osmanieh
(Turkey).

16a. Military Medal.

26a. Foreign Office Medals
(Army L.S. & G.C., old
pattern).

125. Medaille de Sauvetage
(France).

126. Order of the Nile
(Egypt).

THE SOUTH AFRICAN MEDAL (1899-1902)

With Six Bars.   (See No. 78).

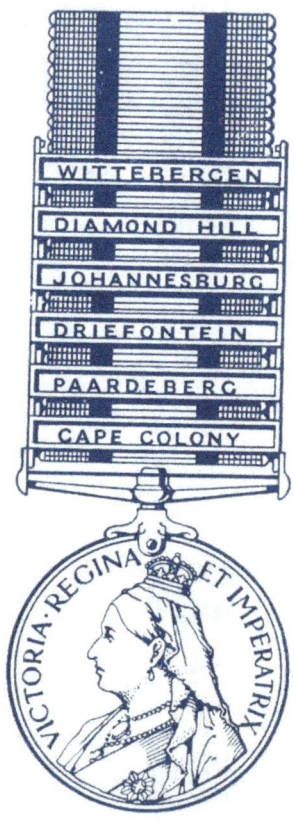

This illustration shows all the parts of a Military Medal, viz., the Ribbon, the Clasp by which the Medal itself is suspended, and the Bars bearing the names of the Campaigns or Battles for which they were conferred.

RIBBONS AND MEDALS

INTRODUCTION

THERE is generally a certain amount of mystification attached to the strips of coloured ribbon worn on the breasts of their undress uniforms by the officers and men of His Majesty's fighting forces and the police. People usually associate the pieces of coloured silk with Orders, Decorations, and Medals, but comparatively few of them can distinguish between the different varieties by a mere glance at the ribbons.

Most of them have their distinctive colourings, and though it is true that many decorations may be won in times of peace, a tolerably complete summary of a man's fighting career may often be obtained by noting the coloured strips of silk on his coat or tunic.

A certain amount of difficulty necessarily exists where there are several ribbons of the same, or much the same, colour. For instance, the Victoria Cross (Army), the Order of the Bath, the French Legion of Honour, and the Army Long Service and Good Conduct Medal,* among others, all have plain red or crimson ribbons of varying shades. The Victoria Cross (Navy), the Khedive's Bronze Star, 1882–91, the Meritorious Service Medal for the Royal Marines, the Royal Humane Society's Medal for saving life, and the Medals given to the police for the Jubilees of 1887 and 1897, too, are all suspended from ribbons of a plain blue of varying shades.

When the actual decorations themselves are being worn their identification is more or less easy, but with the ribbons alone their purport, if they are of the same, or much the same, colour, can only be deduced from their relative positions on a man's breast.

It is laid down that British subjects shall wear the ribbons of their Orders, Decorations, and Medals in a certain sequence on their left breasts, the position of priority being in the centre of the chest. Medals awarded by Societies for saving life, moreover, are worn on the right breast.

The sequence laid down is as follows:—

1. The Victoria Cross.
2. British Orders.
3. British Medals.
4. Foreign Orders in order of date.
5. Foreign Medals in order of date.

---

* In June, 1916, the colour of the ribbon for the Army Long Service and Good Conduct Medal was altered to crimson with white edges. See p. 65.

B

Thus, if it so happened that a British Army officer was the possessor of the Victoria Cross, the Companionship of the Bath, some British war medals, and the Legion of Honour, he would have no less than three crimson, or very nearly crimson, ribbons on his left breast. If you were facing him the dark crimson ribbon of the V.C. would be on the left, *i.e.* towards the centre. Next to it would come the lighter crimson ribbon of the C.B.; then the ribbons of the British war medals; and lastly, the scarlet watered ribbon of the Legion of Honour.

Again, to take dark blue ribbons. A strip of silk of this colour worn on the right breast means the silver or bronze medal of the Royal Humane Society, while one of a similar colour on the left breast may be either the Naval Victoria Cross, the Royal Marine Meritorious Service Medal, the Kaisar-i-Hind Medal, Queen Victoria's Police Jubilee Medal for 1887 or 1897, or the Khedive's Bronze Star for Egypt, 1889 to 1891.

The V.C., as usual, would be worn first, while the Khedive's Star, being a foreign decoration, would be worn on the outside of any British medals the wearer possessed, added to which the Bronze Star is very rarely seen except in conjunction with the British medal for the Egyptian campaigns, with its blue and white striped ribbon.

But even so it is still very easy for the ribbons of the Army and Navy V.Cs. to be mistaken for those of decorations of lesser importance.

The ribbons of the Orders of the Garter, Thistle, and St. Patrick are not worn in undress uniform, while the Order of Merit, with its bi-coloured crimson and blue ribbon and its red enamelled cross, is worn round the neck on all occasions.

The British Orders take precedence as follows :—

1. The Most Noble Order of the Garter.
2. The Most Noble and Most Ancient Order of the Thistle.
3. The Most Illustrious Order of St. Patrick.
4. The Most Honourable Order of the Bath.
5. The Order of Merit.
6. The Most Exalted Order of the Star of India.
7. The Most Distinguished Order of St. Michael and St. George.
8. The Most Eminent Order of the Indian Empire.
9. The Royal Victorian Order: 1st, 2nd, 3rd, and 4th classes.
10. The Distinguished Service Order.
11. The Imperial Service Order.
12. The Royal Victorian Order, 5th class.
13. The Order of British India (for natives of India).
14. The Indian Order of Merit.
15. The Order of St. John of Jerusalem in England.

If, however, an officer possesses the higher grade of a junior Order and the lower grade of a senior Order, the higher grade ribbon comes first, *i.e.* the ribbon of a K.C.I.E. would come before that of a C.B., and that of a G.C.M.G. before that of a K.C.B., etc.

In undress uniform Knights Grand Cross, Knights Grand Commanders, and Commanders of the various Orders wear the ribbons of Companions. In other words, a G.C.B. wears the ribbon of a C.B.; a K.C.S.I. the ribbon of a C.S.I.; a K.C.M.G. the ribbon of a C.M.G.; and a G.C.V.O. the ribbon of an M.V.O. The different grades of the various British Orders are dealt with in the earlier pages of this book.

Generally speaking, anything which is not an Order or a medal is usually held to be a " Decoration." The Victoria Cross, Distinguished Service Cross, Military Cross, Volunteer and Territorial Officers' Decorations, and the Royal Naval Reserve and R.N. Volunteer Reserve Officers' Decorations are cases in point.

Medals fall naturally into four distinct groups :

1. Commemoration medals.
2. Medals for gallantry in action, or for saving life in peace.
3. Medals for war service.
4. Medals for long service and good conduct.

In the first group come the Jubilee, Coronation, and Delhi Durbar medals, and these are worn immediately after Orders. The only exception to this is the Union of South Africa Commemoration Medal, which is worn after long service and good conduct medals.

Among the medals for gallantry in action are the Distinguished Conduct Medal for the Army and the Military Medal; their counterparts, the Conspicuous Gallantry Medal for the Navy; and the newly instituted Naval Distinguished Service Medal. These, all given for war service, are worn immediately before war medals. The Albert Medals, the Board of Trade Medal for saving life at sea, and the Edward Medal, all of which may be awarded for gallantry in saving life at any time, are worn after war medals.

Long service and good conduct medals, which are given to the men of the Navy, Army, Territorial, Yeomanry, and Colonial forces ; and the Naval Good Shooting medals, take precedence after the Albert Medal, Board of Trade Medal, etc.

Medals for war service were not issued generally to all the officers and men engaged until well into the nineteenth century, the only exception in Great Britain being the medal for the Battle of Dunbar, 1650, which was awarded by the vote of the House of Commons to all officers and men of the Parliamentary forces who had been present at the battle.

Throughout the Peninsula War (1808–14) medals were only conferred upon senior officers, and it was not until 1848, by which time many of the veterans had died natural deaths, that the Military General Service medal, with bars for the Peninsula actions, etc., were issued to the surviving junior officers and men for their share in the various engagements. It seems strange to think that participants in battles like Maida, July 4th, 1806, or Albuera, May 11th, 1811, went unrewarded for forty-two and thirty-seven years respectively.

The only exception to this was the Battle of Waterloo, 1815, for a medal was issued in 1817 to all officers and men who had taken part in it.

The Navy suffered in much the same way, for though, for Lord Howe's victory over the French off Ushant, on June 1st, 1794—" the Glorious First of June "—the admirals and captains engaged were rewarded with gold medals, a custom which obtained in all subsequent naval actions except Copenhagen, the junior officers and men received no such distinction till 1848, when the Naval General Service Medal, with, among many others, a bar for " June 1st, 1794," was issued.

After the Battle of the Nile—August 1st, 1798—Lord Nelson's Prize Agent, a Mr. Davison, issued a medal at his own expense to every officer and man engaged. It was given in gold to admirals and captains, in silver to lieutenants and warrant officers, in bronze-gilt to petty officers, and in bronze to the seamen and marines. They were bestowed privately, but were worn and highly prized by their recipients, while the gift cost the donor the best part of £2000.

For the Battle of Trafalgar, too, a Mr. Boulton of Birmingham requested and received the necessary permission to strike and present a medal to every British officer and man engaged on October 21st, 1805. They were given in gold to admirals, in silver to captains and lieutenants, and in pewter to junior officers and men. Mr. Davison, also, gave a special Trafalgar medal in pewter to the officers and ship's company of Lord Nelson's flagship H.M.S. *Victory*.

According to modern ideas it is surprising to think that it was left for private individuals to reward officers and men who had taken a gallant part in such great and far-reaching victories as the Battles of the Nile and Trafalgar, but no official medal with bars for these battles was issued until 1848, just fifty and forty-three years after they had been fought !

It was in the 'forties of the nineteenth century that it became customary to grant a medal to all officers and men who had taken part in a campaign. At first the rather awkward expedient was adopted of inscribing the name of each important battle on the medal itself, and, as a case in point, we may mention the Candahar, Ghuznee, and Cabul medals of 1842, all given for the same war in Afghanistan. They were worded on the REVERSE, or back, " Candahar 1842," " Ghuznee. Cabul 1842," " Candahar. Ghuznee. Cabul. 1842," or " Cabul 1842," and, as a consequence, a casual inspection of a recipient's medal, worn OBVERSE to the front, would not reveal whether, for instance, he was the possessor of the Cabul medal, or the one for Candahar, Ghuznee, and Cabul, to earn which he must have seen far more fighting. The system, therefore, was far from satisfactory.

The medals for the Sutlej campaign, 1845–6, all bore the name of a battle on the reverse, and an officer or man who fought in any one engagement received the appropriate medal. For each subsequent battle he received a bar, a silver bar-shaped attachment worn on the ribbon, and inscribed with the name of the engagement.

For the Punjab campaign, 1848–9, however, the medal without a bar was given to all men who served in the Punjab province, *i.e.* those who were within the sphere of operations, between certain dates. Those who had taken part in the three principal battles, " Chilianwala," " Mooltan," and " Goojerat," received, in addition to the medal, bars so worded.

This is the system which now obtains, except that in some more modern medals the bars bear dates to cover the periods during which the recipients were on active service, instead of the names of battles or places. See the South African medal for 1877 to 1879.

Dated bars, " South Africa 1901," and " South Africa 1902," were issued with Queen Victoria's and King Edward's medals for that campaign to those who qualified for them, while others inscribed " Natal," " Cape Colony," " Orange Free State," or " Transvaal," were given with the Queen's medal to those officers and men who had served in the territories named within certain dates, but who had not received a bar for a specific engagement fought in that territory. The bars mentioned, therefore, could be earned without actual fighting.

What are known as " General Service Medals " were first instituted to obviate the multiplication of medals. In other words, the same medal was given for all small wars or expeditions in a certain country or continent, while bars attached to the ribbon denoted the particular service for which the medal was awarded. When we come to count the number of different medals issued for wars in India between about 1839 and 1854, it will be seen that some such expedient was very necessary. Good examples of General Service medals are the " India Medal 1854," the award of which, with twenty-three different bars, continued up till 1895; the East and West Africa Medal, 1887 to 1900; the Africa General Service Medal of 1902; and the recently instituted Naval General Service Medal.

Actual medals themselves are only worn in full dress, and though the men of the navy and army may frequently be seen with their medals and decorations displayed, the officers of either service are seldom seen wearing them in uniform, for full dress, in the navy particularly, is not often worn.

Miniature medals, small reproductions provided by the wearers themselves, are allowed to be worn by officers in uniform, evening dress, and, on special occasions, in plain clothes evening dress. It is not known when the use of these miniatures was authorised by regulation, though photographs of officers taken soon after the Crimean War show them being worn. The earliest miniature medals of all, however, date from about 1817, when officers who had received the Waterloo Medal had small replicas made for their wives to wear.

The custom of wearing ribbons alone in undress seems to have become usual during the late 'fifties.

There is a widespread belief that medals won by fathers may be worn by sons; but there is nothing to support such an idea. It is true, of course, that medals of deceased officers and men, including the Victoria Cross, are usually given to their nearest relatives, but this does not imply that they are to be worn.

It is a punishable offence for soldiers and sailors on the active list to sell or otherwise dispose of their medals and decorations, but men who lose them accidentally are usually allowed to purchase duplicates.

British subjects are not allowed to accept and wear foreign Orders and medals without first obtaining His Majesty's sanction, but no permission is necessary to accept a foreign medal if such medal is not to be worn. Permission to accept and wear foreign decorations is only granted, as a rule, in cases where they have been earned during war, or for saving life.

In various books and official documents on the subject the engagement bars worn on the ribbons of medals are variously referred to as " bars " or " clasps." Throughout this small volume the term " bar " is used to describe the silver inscribed bar worn on the ribbon; and " clasp " the means by which the medal is suspended from its ribbon.

The " obverse " of a medal, too, is the front, or side worn uppermost; and the " reverse," the back.

The illustrations accompanying the letterpress throughout this book are not all drawn to the same scale. The stars of Orders are shown smaller than the medals, though the originals are considerably larger. The proportionate size of the medals has been increased to show details of design. In actuality, the greater number of British medals are the same size as a five-shilling piece.

DECORATIONS, ORDERS AND MEDALS, AND THE RIBBONS APPERTAINING THERETO, ARE TO BE WORN IN THE FOLLOWING ORDER.

British Decorations, Orders and Medals.

1. Victoria Cross.
2. Order of the Garter.*
3. Order of the Thistle.*
4. Order of St. Patrick.*
5. Order of the Bath.
6. Order of Merit (immediately after Knights Grand Cross of the Bath).†
7. Order of the Star of India.
8. Order of St. Michael and St. George.
9. Order of the Indian Empire.
10. Royal Victorian Order (1st, 2nd, 3rd, and 4th Class).
11. Distinguished Service Order.
12. Imperial Service Order.
13. Royal Victorian Order (5th Class).
14. Order of British India.
15. Indian Order of Merit (Military). ‡
16. Kaiser-i-hind Medal.
17. Order of St. John of Jerusalem in England.
18. Queen Victoria's Jubilee Medal, 1887. (Gold, Silver, and Bronze.)
19. Queen Victoria's Police Jubilee Medal, 1887.
20. Queen Victoria's Jubilee Medal, 1897. (Gold, Silver, and Bronze.)
21. Queen Victoria's Police Jubilee Medal, 1897.
22. Queen Victoria's Commemoration Medal, 1900. (Ireland.)
23. King Edward's Coronation Medal.
24. King Edward's Police Coronation Medal.
25. King Edward's Durbar Medal. (Gold, Silver, and Bronze.)
26. King's Medal, 1903. (Ireland.)
27. King George's Coronation Medal.
28. King George's Police Coronation Medal.
29. King's Visit Commemoration Medal, 1911. (Ireland.)
30. King George's Durbar Medal. (Gold, Silver, and Bronze.)
31. Medal for Distinguished Conduct in the Field (Military).
32. Conspicuous Gallantry Medal (Naval).
33. Distinguished Service Cross (Naval).
34. War Medals (in order of date).
35. Arctic Medal, 1815–1855.
36. Arctic Medal, 1876.
37. Antarctic Medal 1901–1903.
38. Constabulary Medal. (Ireland.)
39. Albert Medal.§
40. Board of Trade Medal for Saving Life at Sea.§

41. Indian Order of Merit (Civil).‡
42. Edward Medal.
43. Indian Distinguished Service Medal.
44. King's Police Medal.
45. Long Service and Good Conduct Medal.
46. Naval Long Service and Good Conduct Medal.
47. Medal for Meritorious Service.
48. Indian Long Service and Good Conduct Medal (for Europeans of Indian Army).
49. Indian Meritorious Service Medal (for Europeans of Indian Army).
50. Royal Marine Meritorious Service Medal.
51. Indian Long Service and Good Conduct Medal (for Native Army).
52. Indian Meritorious Service Medal (for Native Army).
53. Volunteer Officers' Decoration.
54. Volunteer Long Service Medal.
55. Volunteer Officers' Decoration for India and the Colonies.
56. Volunteer Long Service Medal for India and the Colonies.
57. Colonial Auxiliary Forces Officers' Decoration.
58. Colonial Auxiliary Forces Long Service Medal.
59. Medal for Good Shooting (Naval).
60. Militia Long Service Medal.
61. Imperial Yeomanry Long Service Medal.
62. Territorial Efficiency Medal.
63. Territorial Decoration.
64. Special Reserve Long Service and Good Conduct Medal.
65. Decoration for Officers of the Royal Naval Reserve.
66. Decoration for Officers of the Royal Naval Volunteer Reserve.
67. Royal Naval Reserve Long Service and Good Conduct Medal.
68. Royal Naval Volunteer Reserve Long Service Medal.
69. Union of South Africa Commemoration Medal.
70. Royal Victorian Medal. (Gold and Silver.)
71. Imperial Service Medal.
72. Medal of the Order of St. John of Jerusalem in England.§
73. Badge of the Order of the League of Mercy.
74. Royal Victorian Medal. (Bronze.)

---

* These orders are not worn in miniature

† Order of Merit comes immediately after G.C.B., it is not worn in miniature, but is to be worn round the neck on *all* occasions.

‡ The Indian Order of Merit (Military and Civil) is distinct from the Order of Merit instituted in 1902.

§ If more than one of these medals is awarded for the same act of gallantry, only one medal may be worn, *viz.*, that which appears highest in the list.

The Distinguished Service Medal (Naval) is worn after No. 33.

The Military Medal is worn immediately before all war medals.

* THE MOST NOBLE ORDER OF THE GARTER.—This Order, established by King Edward III., in 1348, is the premier Order of Great Britain, and is one of the most ancient in Europe. It comprises twenty-six Knights only, included in which number are the Sovereign, H.M. the Queen, and the Prince of Wales. Extra Knights may be admitted by special statutes.

The insignia of the Order comprises :—

A Garter of dark blue velvet and gold, bearing the motto " Honi soit qui mal y pense " in golden letters. It is worn by H.M. the Queen on the left arm above the elbow, and by Knights on the left leg below the knee.

A Mantle of blue velvet lined with taffeta, with the star of the Order embroidered on the left breast.

A Hood of crimson velvet.

A Surcoat of crimson velvet, lined with white taffeta.

A Hat of black velvet lined with white taffeta, and fastened thereto by a band of diamonds, a plume of white ostrich and black heron's feathers.

A Collar of gold, composed of alternate buckled garters, each encircling a red enamelled rose, and knots of cords enamelled white.

The George, an enamelled figure of St. George fighting the dragon, suspended from the Collar.

The Lesser George, or Badge, similar to " the George," but encircled by an oval garter bearing the motto, and worn on the right hip from a broad, dark blue ribbon passing over the left shoulder.

The Star, a silver, eight-pointed star, bearing in its centre the red cross of St. George on a white ground, surrounded by the garter and motto, and worn on the left breast.

The Garter, Mantle, Hood, Surcoat, Hat, Collar, and George are only worn on special occasions, or when commanded by the Sovereign. In ordinary full dress a Knight of the Garter wears the Lesser George and Star only. The ribbon of the Order is not worn in undress uniform. At death the insignia of the Order are returned by the Knight's nearest male relative. The Star of the Order of the Garter is used as a regimental badge by the Coldstream Guards.

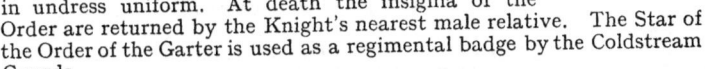

What we may call the " full dress insignia " of the highest classes of the various British Orders of Knighthood, *i.e.* Collars, Mantles, Hoods, Surcoat, Hats, etc., are only worn on special occasions, or when commanded by the Sovereign.

In full dress uniform on ordinary occasions Knights of the Garter, Thistle, and St. Patrick ; Knights Grand Cross of the Bath, St. Michael and St. George, and the Royal Victorian Order ; or Knights Grand Commanders of the Star of India and the Indian Empire, wear the stars of their respective Orders on the left breast, and the badge on one hip from a broad ribbon passing over the opposite shoulder.

Knights of the Garter and Thistle wear their ribbon over the left shoulder, with the badge on the right hip ; while Knights of St. Patrick,

THE MOST NOBLE AND MOST ANCIENT ORDER OF THE THISTLE.—This Order, supposed to have been created in 787 A.D., was revived in 1687 by King James II., and was re-established by Queen Anne, December 31st, 1703. It now consists of the Sovereign and sixteen Knights.

The insignia of the Order comprises :—

A Star, consisting of a silver star in the shape of a St. Andrew's Cross, with other rays issuing between the points of the cross, and in the centre, on a gold background, a thistle enamelled in proper colours surrounded by a green circle bearing the motto, " Nemo Me impune Lacessit " in gold letters, worn on the left breast.

A Collar of gold of alternate thistles and sprigs of rue enamelled in proper colours.

A Mantle of green velvet bound with taffeta, and tied with cords and tassels of green and gold, and having on its left side a figure of St. Andrew bearing his Cross, surrounded by a circlet of gold bearing the motto of the Order.

The Badge or Jewel, a golden image of St. Andrew in green gown and purple surcoat, bearing before him the Cross, enamelled white, the whole surrounded by rays of gold. This is worn pendant from the Collar, or on the right hip from a dark green ribbon passing over the left shoulder.

In ordinary full dress the Star, Badge, and ribbon alone are worn, the Collar and Mantle being used on special occasions, or when ordered by the Sovereign. The ribbon of the Order is not worn in undress uniform. At death the insignia of the Order are returned. Among other regiments, the Scots Guards, Royal Scots, Royal Scots Fusiliers, and Black Watch, incorporate portions of the insignia of the Order of the Thistle on their colours, badges, or appointments.

THE MOST ILLUSTRIOUS ORDER OF ST. PATRICK.—This Order was instituted by King George III. in 1783, and now consists of the Sovereign, the Lord-Lieutenant of Ireland, and twenty-two Knights; also certain Extra and Honorary Knights.

The insignia of the Order comprises :—

A Star : A silver, eight-pointed star, having in its centre, on a white field, the Cross of St. Patrick in red enamel charged with a green trefoil, bearing a crown on each leaf,

---

and Knights Grand Cross or Grand Commanders of other Orders vice versa.

The Collar and Ribbon of an Order are never worn together.

In undress uniform, when ribbons alone are being worn, members of the superior grades of Orders wear the ribbons of Companions, *i.e.*, for instance, in undress a G.C.S.I. would wear the 1½ inch ribbon of a C.S.I. sewn on his coat.

The ribbons of the Garter, Thistle, and St. Patrick are not worn in undress.

surrounded by a sky-blue enamel circle inscribed with the motto, "Quis Separabit," and the date "MDCCLXXXIII."

A Mantle of sky-blue satin made in Ireland, lined with white silk, and on the right shoulder a hood of the same. The Mantle is fastened by a silk cord of blue and gold, and it has the star of the Order embroidered on the right side.

The Collar, of gold, composed of five roses and six harps alternately, each tied together with a knot of gold. The roses are enamelled alternately, white leaves within red, and red within white. In the centre of the Collar is a golden harp surmounted by an Imperial Crown, and from this hangs *the Badge*, similar to the central device of the star, but oval in shape, and surrounded by a wreath of trefoil.

In ordinary full dress the Star and Badge alone are worn, the latter being suspended on the left hip from a sky-blue ribbon two inches wide, passing over the right shoulder. At death the insignia of the Order are returned by the Knight's nearest male relative. The ribbon of the Order is not worn in undress uniform. The Star of the Order of St. Patrick is worn as a regimental badge by the Irish Guards.

THE ROYAL ORDER OF VICTORIA AND ALBERT. FOR LADIES ONLY.—This Order was first instituted in 1862, and now comprises the Sovereign and 45 ladies. It is divided into four classes, the first and second of which are composed entirely of royal personages, foreign as well as British. The third class is composed of titled ladies, or "Honourables." The badge of the 1st and 2nd classes consists of an onyx cameo with the busts of Queen Victoria and the Prince Consort, surmounted by an Imperial crown, the 1st class badge being set in diamonds, and that of the 2nd class in pearls. The 3rd and 4th class badges are fashioned in the form of a monogram, "V & A" set with jewels. The ribbon from which the badges are suspended is worn on the left shoulder in the form of a bow, and is white moiré $1\frac{1}{2}$ inches wide.

THE IMPERIAL ORDER OF THE CROWN OF INDIA. FOR LADIES ONLY.—This Order, instituted on January 1st, 1878, consists " of the Sovereign, and of such of the Princesses of His Majesty's Royal and Imperial House, the wives or other female relatives of Indian Princes, and other Indian ladies, and of the wives of other female relatives of any of the persons who have held, now hold, or may hereafter hold, the office of Viceroy and Governor-General of India, Governors of Madras or Bombay, or of Principal Secretary of State for India, as the Sovereign may think fit to appoint." The badge consists of the Royal and Imperial monogram in diamonds, turquoises, and pearls. It is surrounded by an oval border of pearls, and is surmounted by a jewelled Imperial crown. It is worn on the left shoulder hung from a bow of light-blue watered ribbon, edged white.

* **1** (Navy), **2** (Army). THE VICTORIA CROSS.—The Victoria Cross, the most highly coveted decoration which it is possible for any sailor or soldier, officer or man, to obtain, was instituted by Queen

* Figures in heavy type refer to the coloured representations of ribbons.

Victoria in 1856 at, it is said, the suggestion of the Prince Consort. The decoration consists of a bronze cross pattée, one and a half inches across with raised edges. On the obverse, in the centre, is a lion passant gardant standing upon the Royal crown, while below the crown are the words, "For Valour," on a semicircular scroll. The reverse has raised edges like the obverse, while the date of the act for which the decoration is bestowed is engraved in a circle in the centre. The Cross is suspended by means of a plain link from a V, which is part and parcel of the clasp, ornamented with laurel leaves, through which the ribbon passes, and on the back of this clasp is engraved the name, rank and ship or regiment of the recipient. The ribbon, one and a half inches wide, is blue for the Royal Navy, and crimson for the Army. The V.C. was established during the Crimean War as a means of rewarding individual officers and men of the Navy and Army who might perform some signal act of valour or devotion to their country in the presence of the enemy, and clasps attached to the ribbon might be

I, 2.

awarded for any subsequent acts of gallantry. If, also, the recipients were below the rank of commissioned officers, the Cross was to be accompanied by a pension of £10 a year, with an additional £5 per annum for each bar. In 1898, however, it was ordered that the £10 per annum might be increased to £50 in cases where the recipients were in very reduced circumstances. Any one who has received the V.C., but who is afterwards convicted of treason, cowardice, felony, or of any other infamous crime, may have his name erased from the list of recipients. In 1857 the European officers and men in the East India Company's Service were declared eligible for the decoration; while in 1858 it was ordained that cases of great bravery performed NOT in the presence of the enemy were admissible. The only case on record, however, where the V.C. was granted in the latter circumstances was in 1867, when it was bestowed on Private Timothy O'Hea, of the 1st Battalion of the Rifle Brigade, for his courageous behaviour in helping to extinguish a fire in an ammunition railway car during the Fenian Raid in Canada, 1866. In 1858 the award of the Cross was extended to civilians who had distinguished themselves during the Indian Mutiny, while in 1867 the officers and men of the Colonial Forces were also declared to be eligible. In 1881 the qualification for the decoration was again defined to be "conspicuous bravery or devotion to the country in the presence of the enemy," while officers and men of the auxiliary and reserve forces, Navy and Army, and Chaplains, were also declared eligible. The first distribution of the Victoria Cross was made on June 26th, 1856, when Queen Victoria personally decorated sixty-one recipients. Fourteen of these belonged to the Royal Navy, and forty-seven to the Army. In 1902 King Edward issued an order to the effect that Victoria Crosses earned by soldiers and sailors who had been killed should be delivered to the relatives. Previous to this date, when officers or men had been recommended for the V.C., but had died before their bestowal, the recipients' names appeared in the official *Gazette*, but the decoration was never actually conferred. The order was made retrospective, so that surviving relatives of men who had won the Cross so far back as in the Crimean War, or the Indian Mutiny, but had died whilst performing their gallant deeds, received the coveted token. During the present war many Victoria Crosses have been given posthumously. In 1912 King George V. extended the award of the Victoria Cross to native officers and men of the Indian Army, who up to that time had only been eligible for the Indian Order of Merit for gallant deeds in action. The Victoria Cross is the rarest of all British decorations, and takes precedence of all other Orders and medals. One of the very few instances of a bar being added to the V.C. occurred during the present war, when Captain Arthur Martin Leake, R.A.M.C., who had received the Cross during the Boer War, was awarded a bar for another act of bravery during the present campaign.*

3. THE MOST HONOURABLE ORDER OF THE BATH.— The Order of the Bath was founded in 1399, and was revived by King George I. in 1725. The Order is divided into a military division and a civil division, and there are three classes in each, viz. Knights Grand Cross (G.C.B.); Knights Commander (K.C.B.); and Companion (C.B.). The C.B. of the military division is only conferred upon officers of or above the rank of Commander in the Navy, or Major in the Army, who have been mentioned in despatches for services in war, and they may subsequently be advanced to the higher grades of the Order. The civil C.B. may be bestowed upon officers of both Services in times of peace, and upon civilians. The following are the insignia of the Order:—

The Collar of gold, composed of nine crowns and eight devices, each consisting of a rose, a thistle, and a shamrock, issuing from a sceptre, all enamelled in their proper colours. The crowns and devices are linked together with gold, white enamelled knots. From the Collar hangs

The Badge. The Military Badge consists of a gold Maltese cross of eight points, enamelled white. Each point is tipped with a small gold ball, and in each angle between the arms of the cross is a gold lion. In the centre of the cross is a device consisting of the rose, thistle, and shamrock, issuing from a sceptre, and three imperial crowns. This device is surrounded by a red enamel circle, on which is the motto of the Order, " Tria juncta in uno," in gold letters. The

3. Military Badge.

circle is again surrounded by two branches of laurel, enamelled green, and below is a blue enamel scroll with the words " Ich Dien " in gold letters.

The Civil Badge is of gold filigree work, and is oval in shape. It consists of a bandlet bearing the motto, and in the centre is the usual device of the rose, thistle, and shamrock issuing from a sceptre, and the three crowns.

A Knight Grand Cross (G.C.B.) wears the Collar on special occasions only. On ordinary full dress occasions he wears the badge (military or civil, as the case may be) on the left hip, suspended from a broad crimson ribbon passing over the right shoulder.

3. Civil Badge.

He wears, in addition, a Star on the left breast.

* See page 78.

Star of Military G.C.B.—A gold Maltese cross of the same pattern as the military Badge, mounted on a silver flaming star.

Star of Civil G.C.B.—A silver, eight-pointed star, with a central device of three crowns upon a silver ground, encircled by the motto on a red enamel riband.

3. Star.
Military G.C.B.

A Knight Commander (K.C.B.) wears a smaller sized badge (military or civil, as the case may be) suspended round the neck from a crimson ribbon, and, in addition, a star on the left breast.

Star of Military K.C.B.—A similar star to that of a military G.C.B., but with the gold Maltese cross omitted, and the star itself in the shape of a silver cross pattée.

Star of Civil K.C.B.—Similar to that of a Military K.C.B., but without a laurel wreath.

A Companion of the Order (C.B.) wears a smaller sized badge (military or civil, as the case may be) on the left breast, suspended from a crimson ribbon (No. 3) with a gold buckle halfway up the ribbon.

3. Star.
Military K.C.B.

The gold and enamel military badges were not instituted until 1815, before which date they were exactly the same as the present-day civil badges. The civil branch of the Order was established in 1847. The C.B. does not carry with it the honour of Knighthood, as does the K.C.B. or G.C.B.

In undress uniform a G.C.B. or a K.C.B. wears the ribbon of a C.B., and in mess dress the miniature badge of a C.B. without the buckle.

4. ORDER OF MERIT.—This Order was instituted in 1902, and is awarded very rarely to officers of both Services and to civilians for very distinguished and conspicuous services either in peace or in war. The badge consists of a gold cross, pattée convexed, enamelled red, edged blue, with, in the centre of the obverse, the words " For Merit " on a blue ground. In the centre of the reverse is the Royal Cypher. The cross is surmounted by a Tudor crown, and is worn round the neck from a ribbon, half blue, half crimson, of two inches in width. Naval or military recipients of the Order have two silver crossed swords between the arms of the cross in their badge, but in the case of civilian recipients the swords are omitted. Those who have received the Order of Merit have the right to use the letters " O.M. " after their names.

4.

The badge is not worn in miniature, neither is the ribbon sewn on the coat, for the regulations lay down that officers in uniform are to wear it round the neck on all occasions.

5. THE MOST EXALTED ORDER OF THE STAR OF INDIA. —This Order was instituted by Queen Victoria in 1861, and the dignity of Knight Grand Commander (G.C.S.I.) can be conferred upon Princes or Chiefs of India, or upon British subjects, for important and loyal services rendered to the Indian Empire. The second and third classes of the Order (K.C.S.I. and C.S.I.) are bestowed for similar services of not less than thirty years' duration. The Order consists of the Sovereign; a Grand Master (the Viceroy of India); 36 Knights Grand Commanders (18 British and 18 Native); 85 Knights Commander (K.C.S.I.); and 170 Companions (C.S.I.). The Badge of the Order is an onyx cameo bearing the effigy of Queen Victoria, set in a perforated, ornamental oval containing the motto of the Order —" Heaven's Light our Guide "—in diamonds, surmounted by a star, also in diamonds.

5. Badge.

The insignia of a G.C.S.I. consists of a gold Collar, formed of lotus flowers, palm branches, and united red and white roses, from which the Badge is suspended. A Star, consisting of golden rays issuing from a centre, having thereon a diamond star resting upon a circular riband of light blue enamel, bearing the motto in diamonds, and a Mantle of light blue satin with a representation of the star on the left side, and tied with a white silk cord with blue and silver tassels. The Collar and Mantle, however, are only worn on special occasions, and in ordinary full dress uniform a G.C.S.I. wears the Star on the left breast, and the Badge on the left hip from a broad light blue, white edged ribbon or sash passing over the right shoulder.

5. Star.

A *K.C.S.I.* wears the Badge round his neck from a ribbon two inches wide, and a Star—similar to that of a G.C.S.I., but in silver—on the left breast.

A *C.S.I.* wears the badge on his left breast from a ribbon one and a half inches wide.

N.B.—In undress uniform G.C.S.I.'s and K.C.S.I.'s wear the ribbons of a C.S.I.

6. THE MOST DISTINGUISHED ORDER OF ST. MICHAEL AND ST. GEORGE.—This Order was founded in 1818 by King George III., and is usually conferred upon British subjects as a reward for services abroad or in the Colonies. The Order is divided into three classes: Knights Grand Cross (G.C.M.G.); Knights Commander (K.C.M.G.); and Companions (C.M.G.). The insignia of the Order is as follows :—

The Collar of gold, formed alternately of lions of England, of Maltese crosses in white enamel, and of the cyphers S.M. and S.G., with, in the centre, two winged lions, each holding a book and seven arrows.

6. Badge.

The Badge is a gold seven-pointed star with V-shaped extremities, enamelled white and edged gold, surmounted by the Imperial Crown. In the centre, on one side is a representation in enamel of St. Michael

encountering Satan, and, on the other, St. George on horseback fighting the dragon. This device is surrounded by a circle of blue enamel, bearing the motto, " Auspicium Melioris Ævi," in gold.

The Mantle is of Saxon blue, lined with scarlet silk, tied with cords of blue and scarlet silk and gold, and having on the left side the star of the Order.

The Chapeau, or Hat, is of blue satin, lined with scarlet, and surmounted by black and white ostrich feathers.

6. G.C.M.G. Star.

Knights Grand Cross (G.C.M.G.) are entitled to wear the Collar, Mantle, and Chapeau on special occasions, or when commanded by the Sovereign; but in ordinary full dress wear the Badge on the left hip from a broad ribbon, Saxon blue, with a central scarlet stripe, passing over the right shoulder. They wear, in addition, a Star on the left breast. This is a silver star of seven rays, with a gold ray between each, and over all the Cross of St. George in red enamel. In the centre is a representation of St. Michael encountering Satan within a blue circular riband bearing the motto, " Auspicium Melioris Ævi."

Knights Commanders wear the Badge suspended round the neck from a narrower ribbon of the same colours, and, on the left breast, a silver eight-pointed star charged with the red St. George's Cross, and with the same central device as the G.C.M.G. star.

Companions wear the Badge on the left breast from a ribbon (No. 6) one and a half inches wide with a gold buckle halfway up the ribbon. In undress uniform Knights Grand Cross and Knights Commanders wear the ribbon of Companions of the Order.

7. Badge.

7. THE MOST EMINENT ORDER OF THE INDIAN EMPIRE.—This Order was instituted by Queen Victoria in 1878, and is divided into three classes : Knights Grand Commander (G.C.I.E.); Knights Commander (K.C.I.E.); and Companions (C.I.E.). The insignia of the Order are :—

The Collar of gold, formed of elephants, lotus flowers, peacocks in their pride, Indian roses, and in the centre the Imperial Crown, the whole linked together with chains.

The Badge, consisting of a gold, five-petalled rose, enamelled crimson, and with a green barb between each petal. In the centre an effigy of Queen Victoria on a gold ground, surrounded by a purple riband, edged and lettered gold, bearing the motto " Imperatricis Auspiciis."

7. Star.

The Mantle of Imperial purple satin, lined with white silk and fastened with a white silk cord with gold tassels, and having on the left side a representation of the Star of the Order.

Knights Grand Commanders are entitled to wear the Mantle, and the Badge, suspended from the Collar, on special occasions, or when ordered by His Majesty. On ordinary full dress occasions they wear the Badge on the left hip, suspended from a broad ribbon of Imperial purple, passing over the left shoulder, and, on the left breast, a Star. This Star is composed of fine rays of silver, having a smaller ray of gold between each, the whole alternately plain and scaled. In the centre, within a purple circle bearing the motto and surmounted by the Imperial Crown in gold, is the effigy of H.M. Queen Victoria on a gold ground.

Knights Commanders wear a smaller sized badge, suspended round the neck from a purple ribbon two inches in width, and on the left breast a star similar to that of Knights Grand Commanders, but with the rays fashioned entirely in silver.

Companions wear a still smaller sized badge on the left breast, suspended from a purple ribbon one and a half inches in width. In undress uniform Knights Grand Commanders and Knights Commanders wear the ribbons of Companions.

The Order of the Indian Empire, as its name implies, is only awarded for services in India.

8. THE ROYAL VICTORIAN ORDER.—The Royal Victorian Order was established by Queen Victoria in April, 1896. There is no limit to the number of members, and the Order, which is conferred for extraordinary, important, or personal services to the Sovereign or to the Royal Family, can be bestowed upon foreigners as well as upon British subjects. The Order is divided into five classes : Knights Grand Cross (G.C.V.O.); Knights Commanders (K.C.V.O.); Commanders (C.V.O.); and Members of the 4th and 5th Classes of the Order (M.V.O.). The Badge consists of a white enamelled Maltese cross of eight points, in the centre of which is an oval of crimson enamel with the cypher " V.R.I." in gold letters. Encircling this is a blue enamel riband with the name " Victoria " in gold letters, and above is the Imperial Crown enamelled in proper colours.

8. Badge.

8. G.C.V.O. Star.

Knights Grand Cross wear the badge on the left hip from a broad ribbon similar to No. 8 hung over the right shoulder, and, on the left breast, a silver chipped star of eight points, with the white enamel badge in the centre.

Knights Commanders have the badge suspended round the neck, and, on the left breast, a silver chipped star in the shape of a Maltese cross with, in its centre, the badge in frosted silver.

Commanders wear the badge suspended round the neck.

Members of the 4th Class of the Order wear the white enamelled badge on the left breast in line with their other orders and medals, while those of the *5th Class* have a similar badge in frosted silver instead of in white enamel. The Royal Victorian Medal, in gold, silver, or bronze, may be awarded to those below the rank of officers who perform personal services to the Sovereign or to members of the Royal Family. The medal bears on the obverse the bust of the reigning Sovereign, with the usual legend, and on the reverse, on an oval lozenge surmounted by scrolls, the Imperial cypher. Below are the words " Royal Victorian

Medal." The medal has the same ribbon as the 4th and 5th Classes of the Order, and, in the case of those bearing the heads of Queen Victoria and King Edward, is surmounted by an Imperial Crown, at the top of which is a ring through which the ribbon passes. The Victorian medals bearing the effigy of King George are without the Imperial Crown, and the ribbon passes through a ring in the top of the medal.

8. K.C.V.O. Star.

A few years ago a Collar was instituted for this Order. It is of gold, with no enamel or colour. The Collar is issued to every Knight Grand Cross, but he is required to deliver it up if he subsequently receives the Grand Cross of a higher Order.

The Royal Victorian Chain is a separate decoration, much smaller than the Collar, and is given to very few individual Knights Grand Cross. It is always worn in full dress, while the Collar can only be worn on "Collar Days." The Royal Victorian Medal is worn on the left breast, after Long Service and Good Conduct Medals.

9.

9.

9. THE DISTINGUISHED SERVICE ORDER. 1886.—The Distinguished Service Order was established in 1886 to reward the distinguished services of officers in the Naval and Military Services of the Empire who have been specially recommended in despatches for meritorious or distinguished service in the field, or before the enemy. Foreign officers who have been associated in naval or military operations with the British forces are also eligible for honorary membership. The badge, worn on the left breast, consists of a gold cross pattée, convexed, enamelled white, edged gold, having on one side in the centre, within a wreath of laurel enamelled green, the Imperial Crown in gold upon a red enamelled ground, and on the reverse, within a similar wreath, and on a similar red ground, the Royal cypher. The badge hangs from the ribbon by a gold clasp ornamented with laurel, while another similar clasp is worn at the top of the ribbon. The D.S.O. ranks immediately after the 4th Class of the Royal Victorian Order, and for officers to be eligible for it they must have been "mentioned in despatches." The number of members of the Order is unlimited.*

10. IMPERIAL SERVICE ORDER. IMPERIAL SERVICE MEDAL.—This Order and Medal were instituted by King Edward in August, 1902, as a means of rewarding meritorious services on the part of members of the administrative or clerical branches of the Civil Service. The number of Companions is not to exceed 700, of whom 250 shall belong to the Home Civil Service; 200 to the Indian Civil Service, including the Staff of the Secretary of State for India (100 appointments being reserved for Europeans, and 100 for natives of India), and 250 to the Civil Services of the Dominions, Colonies, and Protectorates. At least twenty-five years' meritorious service is the

---

* See page 78.

usual qualification for companionship (for Europeans in India is twenty years), or sixteen years in unhealthy places abroad. The Order can, however, be bestowed upon those who have performed, "eminently meritorious service" without the recipients having completed these periods. There is only one class of the Order, and companionship does not carry with it the honour of Knighthood. Companions, however, use the letters "I.S.O." after their names. The badge consists of a circular plaque of gold having in its centre the Royal Cypher, and round its circumference the words "For Faithful Service," both in dark blue lettering. The badge for men is surrounded by a seven-pointed star of silver, surmounted by a crown; while that for women has a silver laurel wreath in place of the star. Members of the Civil

10.

Service who are not eligible for the I.S.O. may be granted the "Imperial Service Medal" under the same conditions as the Order. The medal is the same as the badge of the Order, except that the plaque is of silver, and the star or laurel wreath is of bronze. The name of the recipient also appears on the reverse. Both the Order and Medal have rings for suspension, and are worn by men on the left breast in the ordinary way; and by women on the left shoulder from the ribbon tied in a bow.

11. INDIAN ORDER OF MERIT.—This Order was instituted in 1837 for the purpose of rewarding any conspicuous act of individual gallantry in battle on the part of native officers, non-commissioned officers, or soldiers of the Indian Army. It is quite distinct from the British Order of Merit established by King Edward in 1902. There are three classes of the Order:—

The FIRST CLASS BADGE is an eight-pointed gold star one and a half inches in diameter. In the centre, on a circular ground of dark blue enamel, are two crossed swords in gold within a circle, surrounded by the words "Reward of Valour" in gold. Outside this is a gold laurel wreath. The badge hangs by means of a ring from a gold clasp through which the ribbon passes.

11.

The SECOND CLASS BADGE is a similar star in silver, with the laurel wreath and central device in gold, while it hangs from its ribbon by means of a silver ring and clasp.

The THIRD CLASS BADGE is similar to that of the 2nd Class, but is worked entirely in silver.

Admission to the 3rd Class of the Indian Order of Merit is obtained by any conspicuous act of gallantry in the field on the part of a native officer, non-commissioned officer, or soldier of the Indian Army, without distinction in rank. Admission to the 2nd Class of the Order can only be obtained by members of the 3rd Class for similar services; and only members of the 2nd Class are eligible for the 1st Class in the same circumstances. Members of the 3rd Class receive an increase equal to one-third of their pay, in addition to their pay or pension. Those of the 2nd Class receive an increase equal to two-thirds of their pay; and those of the 1st Class double pay, or full pay, in addition to their ordinary pay or pension.

RIBBON:—1st Class, same as No. 3, but 2 ins. wide.
2nd Class, same as No. 3.

ORDER OF BRITISH INDIA.—This Order was created in 1837, to be conferred on native officers of the Indian Army of the ranks

of Subadar and Jemadar, for long and faithful service. There are two classes of the Order. The 1st consists of 100 Subadars who receive a special allowance of 2 rupees a day in addition to their pay, and the 2nd of 100 native commissioned officers who receive an allowance of 1 rupee a day. Members of the 1st Class, also, receive the title of "Sirdar Bahadoor," and those of the 2nd Class that of "Bahadoor."

Badge, 1st Class.

THE BADGE OF THE FIRST CLASS OF THE ORDER consists of a gold star of eight points, radiated, having at its top the crown of England. In the centre, on a light blue circular field, is a gold lion, and outside this, on a band of dark blue enamel, are the words "Order of British India" in gold letters. The whole of the central device is encircled by a gold laurel wreath, and the badge hangs from its ribbon by means of a gold ring and loop.

THE BADGE OF THE SECOND CLASS is somewhat smaller, and consists of a radiated star of much the same pattern. It has no crown, while the lion in the centre appears on a dark blue field instead of light blue. The method of suspension is the same.

The badges of both classes are worn round the neck from crimson ribbons two inches and one and a half inches wide respectively. It was originally intended that the colour of the ribbon should be sky blue, but this was altered in 1838 to crimson, for, owing to the habit of all classes of natives of oiling their hair, the light ribbon, worn round the neck, would soon be soiled.

12. THE ORDER OF ST. JOHN OF JERUSALEM IN ENGLAND.—It is impossible in the space at our disposal to give a full and

complete account of the work carried on under the auspices of the Grand Priory of the Order of the Hospital of St. John of Jerusalem in England. It is principally concerned with hospital and ambulance work. The St. John of Jerusalem Ambulance Association provides for: (1) The dissemination of instruction in "first aid." (2) Lectures to women on home nursing and hygiene. (3) The deposit in convenient places of stretchers, splints, bandages, etc. (4) The development of Ambulance Corps for the transport of sick and wounded. The Order itself is of very ancient origin, dating from the eleventh century. It has branches in nearly all European countries, and was incorporated in England by Queen Victoria under Royal Charter, May 14th, 1888. We are principally concerned with the various decorations

12.

of the Order which may be worn in public by its members, and the BADGE consists of a true Maltese Cross, embellished alternately in each of its principal angles with a lion guardant and a unicorn, both passant. His Majesty the King is the Sovereign Head and Patron of the Order. Next in authority is the Grand Prior, and this office is now held by H.R.H. the Duke of Connaught.

The HABIT of the GRAND PRIOR consists of a black velvet mantle, embroidered on the left side with the Cross, or badge, of the Order.

The HABIT of the KNIGHTS OF JUSTICE is of black silk, having on the left side the Cross of the Order embellished in gold ; while that of the KNIGHTS OF GRACE is of black camlet with the Cross embellished in silver. The habits described above are only worn on special occasions. At other times the insignia is as follows :—

GRAND PRIOR. The badge or Cross, in white enamel, set in and embellished with gold, surmounted by an Imperial Crown worn round the neck from a black watered silk ribbon,

KNIGHTS OF JUSTICE wear the same badge without the crown, suspended round the neck, while LADIES OF JUSTICE wear it on the left shoulder from a black watered silk ribbon tied in a bow.

CHAPLAINS are not entitled to wear the Habit, but have the same badges as Knights of Justice.

KNIGHTS OF GRACE and LADIES OF GRACE wear white enamel badges in the same way as Knights and Ladies of Justice, respectively, but their badges are set in and embellished with silver.

ESQUIRES wear the white enamel badges, set in and embellished with silver, suspended on the left breast from a black watered silk ribbon.

SERVING BROTHERS AND SISTERS wear the badge on the arm embroidered or stamped in silver.

HONORARY SERVING BROTHERS AND SISTERS wear a badge in the shape of a circular medallion. It consists of the Cross of the Order in white enamel embellished in silver, on a black ground, the whole mounted in silver. Gentlemen wear this badge on the left breast suspended from a black watered silk ribbon, and ladies on the left shoulder from a bow of the same.

HONORARY ASSOCIATES have the badge of the Order in silver, gentlemen wearing it on the left breast suspended from the usual ribbon, and ladies on the left shoulder attached to a bow of the same.

N.B.—The Order of St. John of Jerusalem is essentially aristocratic, and at one time members had to have sixteen quarterings of nobility on their coat of arms. The term " Knights of Justice " originally meant Knights who were noble by birth, while " Knights of Grace " were those of non-noble birth who were admitted to the order for their attainments.

12. MEDAL OF THE ORDER OF ST. JOHN OF JERUSALEM IN ENGLAND.—This medal, in silver and bronze, was originally instituted in 1874, and is awarded for gallantry in saving life on land. It is circular in shape, and bears on the obverse the Cross of the Order surrounded by the legend, " FOR SERVICE IN THE CAUSE OF HUMANITY." The reverse has a sprig of the plant known as St. John's Wort, with which is entwined a scroll bearing the words, " JERUSALEM, ENGLAND," the whole surrounded by the words, " AWARDED BY THE GRAND PRIORY OF THE ORDER OF THE HOSPITAL OF ST. JOHN OF JERUSALEM IN

ENGLAND." The medal hangs from its ribbon by means of a ring ; is worn on the left breast, and can only be awarded to those who, by a conspicuous act of gallantry, have endangered their own lives.

13. THE DISTINGUISHED SERVICE CROSS. (Late Conspicuous Service Cross.)—The Conspicuous Service Cross was instituted

by King Edward in 1901 as a means of " recognising meritorious or distinguished services before the enemy," performed by warrant officers, acting warrant officers, or by subordinate officers (*i.e.* midshipmen, naval cadets, clerks, and assistant clerks) of His Majesty's Fleet. No person could be nominated to the Cross unless his name had been mentioned in despatches, while the award of the Decoration carried with it the right to have the letters " C.S.C." appended to the officer's name. In October, 1914, the name of this Decoration was altered to the " Distinguished Service Cross," and its award was extended to all Naval and Marine officers

13.

below the relative rank of Lieutenant-Commander, " for meritorious or distinguished services which may not be sufficient to warrant the appointment of such officers to the Distinguished Service Order." The letters after a recipient's name, too, were altered to " D.S.C.," while the proviso that a recipient must have been mentioned in despatches still held good. The decoration itself, which is suspended from its ribbon by a ring, is a plain silver cross pattée convexed with the reverse side plain. On the obverse it bears the Imperial cypher of the reigning Sovereign surmounted by the Imperial crown.*

13. THE CONSPICUOUS GALLANTRY MEDAL.—This medal, which is for rewarding petty officers and men of the Royal Navy, and

non-commissioned officers and men of the Royal Marines who may at any time distinguish themselves by acts of conspicuous gallantry in action with the enemy, is the naval counterpart of the Army medal for Distinguished Conduct in the Field. It was originally sanctioned for the Crimean War only, but was reinstituted in 1874, and is now available for any war. The medal is of silver, and has on one side the effigy of the reigning Sovereign with the usual legend, and on the other, in raised letters, the words " For Conspicuous Gallantry," with a crown above, and the whole design encircled by olive branches. Medals

13.

awarded before 1874 had an ornamental scroll clasp for suspension, but those issued since this date have a plain clasp. Petty Officers of the Navy and Sergeants of the Royal Marines may be awarded an annuity not exceeding £20 with this medal, while men of junior grades may be awarded a gratuity of £20 on discharge from the service, or on promotion to a commission.*

---

* See page 78.

14. THE DISTINGUISHED SERVICE MEDAL. 1914.—This
medal was established on October 14th, 1914, during the present war.
It is designed to be awarded in the numerous
cases of courageous service in war by petty officers
and men of the Royal Navy, and non-commissioned officers and men of the Royal Marines, and
all other persons holding corresponding positions
in the naval forces, who "may at any time show
themselves to the fore in action, and set an example of bravery and resource under fire, but
without performing acts of such pre-eminent
bravery as would render them eligible for the
Conspicuous Gallantry Medal." The medal bears
on one side the effigy of King George V. in naval
uniform, with the legend "Georgius V. Britt: Omn:

14.

Rex et Ind: Imp.," and on the reverse the inscription, "For Distinguished Service," surmounted by a crown, and encircled by a wreath of
laurel. It hangs from its ribbon by means of a straight silver clasp.*

15. MILITARY CROSS. 1914.—This decoration was instituted on
December 31st, 1914, during the present war. It is entirely an Army
decoration, and no person is eligible to receive it
unless he is a Captain, a commissioned officer of
a lower grade, or a warrant officer in the Army,
Indian Army, or Colonial Forces. The Cross is
only awarded after recommendation by the Secretary of State for War. The decoration consists of
an ornamental silver cross, on each arm of which is
an Imperial Crown. In the centre is the Imperial
cypher "G.R.I.," and the Cross hangs by its top arm
from the plain silver clasp through which the ribbon
passes. The Military Cross is worn after British
Orders and before war medals, but does not carry
with it any individual precedence.*

15.

16. MEDAL FOR DISTINGUISHED CONDUCT IN THE FIELD.
—A medal for "meritorious service" was instituted
in 1845. It was awarded on the recommendation of
the Commander-in-Chief only to sergeants, while serving or after discharge, with or without a pension.
The Distinguished Conduct Medal, or "D.C.M.," as
it is usually called, is exclusively for the non-commissioned officers and men of the Army, and was
sanctioned in 1854 to replace the old "Meritorious
Service Medal" for gallantry in action. The D.C.M.,
which is suspended from its ribbon by an ornamental
scroll clasp, bears on one side the effigy of the reigning Sovereign, and on the other the inscription "For
Distinguished Conduct in the Field." The date of

16.

the action for which the medal is given is sometimes engraved upon it,
while bars bearing the dates of any subsequent gallant actions may

---

* See page 78.

be awarded. Non-commissioned officers and men who have been given this medal either receive a gratuity of £20 on discharge from the Army, or an increase in pension of 6d. a day.*

16a. THE MILITARY MEDAL.—In March, 1916, His Majesty instituted a new medal to be awarded to non-commissioned officers and men of the Army for individual or associated acts of bravery brought to notice by the recommendation of a Commander-in-Chief in the field. The medal, which is silver, is designated "The Military Medal," and bears on the obverse the Royal Effigy, and on the reverse the words "For Bravery in the Field," encircled by a wreath and surmounted by the Royal Cypher and a Crown. The medal is worn on the left breast immediately before war medals, and its ribbon is dark blue having in the centre three white and two crimson stripes alternating. Men who have been awarded the medal may be granted a bar for further acts of bravery in action.

The grant of this medal, which does not supersede No. 16, the "D.C.M.," places the men of the Army on much the same footing as those in the Navy, who are eligible for the Conspicuous Gallantry Medal, No. 13, and the Distinguished Service Medal, No. 14, for services in action. It may be awarded to women, on the recommendation of a Commander-in-Chief in the field, for devotion to duty under fire.*

17. INDIAN DISTINGUISHED SERVICE MEDAL. 1907.— This medal was instituted by King Edward in 1907 as a means of rewarding the distinguished services of Indian non-commissioned officers and men, and the members of the Military Police and British troops when employed under the orders of the Indian Government. The medal has on one side the effigy of the reigning Sovereign, with the usual legend, and on the other a laurel wreath with the words, "For Distinguished Service." The original Royal Warrant authorising the grant of the medal implies that it may be given for distinguished services in peace as well as in war.

18. ROYAL RED CROSS. 1883.—This decoration consists of a crimson enamelled cross pattée with gold edges, having on its four arms the words "FAITH," "HOPE," "CHARITY," and the date of its institution, "1883." In the centre of the cross is a small bust of the Sovereign in gold on a gold ground. The reverse is plain, but has the Imperial crown and cypher in the centre. The Royal Red Cross, which really corresponds to the D.S.O., was instituted on April 27th, 1883, and is awarded to ladies or nursing sisters who may be recommended for special exertions in attending to sick or wounded sailors or soldiers. It is awarded for services in peace as well as in war, though more rarely. The decoration is suspended by a ring, and is worn on the left shoulder, hanging from the ribbon tied in a bow. Ladies upon whom the Royal Red Cross is conferred have the letters "R.R.C." after their names. This is the first example of a British Military Order for ladies.

18.

His present Majesty has recently instituted another decoration for

---

* See page 78.

ladies. It really comprises the second class of the Royal Red Cross. It is worn from the same ribbon, but the decoration itself is of frosted silver with a Maltese cross of red enamel superimposed. Those ladies upon whom it is conferred have the right to use the letters A.R.R.C. (Associate of the Royal Red Cross) after their names.

19-22. THE ALBERT MEDALS.

    1st Class for gallantry in saving life at sea, No. **19.**
    2nd Class for gallantry in saving life at sea, No. **20.**
    1st Class for gallantry in saving life on land, No. **21.**
    2nd Class for gallantry in saving life on land, No. **22.**

These Decorations, said to have been designed by Prince Albert, were originally established by Queen Victoria in 1866 for distinguishing the " many heroic acts performed by mariners and others who endanger their own lives in saving, or endeavouring to save, the lives of others from shipwrecks and other perils of the sea "; while in 1877 it was also extended for saving life on land for " the many heroic acts performed on land by those who endanger their lives in saving or endeavouring to save the lives of others from accidents in mines, or railways, and at fires, or other peril within Her Dominions, other than perils of the sea." The decorations were known as the " Albert Medal of the First Class," and the " Albert Medal of the Second Class," inscribed " For Gallantry in Saving Life at Sea," and similar decorations inscribed " For Gallantry in Saving Life on Land."

19, 20.

In 1905 the rules for the award of the medals were amended, and it was ordained that the grant of decorations of the 1st Class should be " confined to cases of extreme or heroic daring," and those of the 2nd Class should be given " in cases which, though falling within the cases contemplated by this Warrant, are not sufficiently distinguished to deserve the Albert Medal of the 1st Class." The Albert Medal of the 1st Class for gallantry in saving life at sea consists of an oval gold badge, enamelled in dark blue, with a monogram in the centre composed of the letters " V " and " A " in gold, interlaced with an anchor in gold. The badge is encircled by a bronze garter, inscribed in raised gold letters, " For Gallantry in Saving Life at Sea," and is surmounted by a representation in bronze of the crown of H.R.H. the late Prince Consort. At the top of the crown there is a ring through which the ribbon, No. 19, passes. The medal of the 2nd Class, for gallantry in saving life at sea, is worked entirely in bronze, instead of in gold and bronze, and is suspended from ribbon No. 20. The Albert Medal of the 1st Class for gallantry in saving life on land is the same as that of the 1st Class for saving life at sea, except that the decoration is enamelled crimson, the anchor is omitted, and the inscription reads " For Gallantry in Saving Life on Land," Its ribbon is shown in Fig. 21. That of the 2nd Class for gallantry in saving life on land (Ribbon No. 22) is of exactly the same design, but is worked entirely in bronze. In 1904 the 2nd Class ribbons were increased in width from $\frac{7}{8}''$ to $1\frac{3}{8}''$ (Nos. 20 and 22). Any subsequent act of gallantry which is considered worthy of recognition by the award of the Albert Medal may be recorded by a bar. It is ordained, further, that any recipient of the Albert Medal who may be guilty of any crime or disgraceful conduct shall have his name erased from the register of recipients, and shall be required to return the decoration. Every person on receiving the Medal, moreover, is required to enter into an engagement to return it if his name is so erased. The Albert Medals are extremely rare. In 1913 Chief Stoker William Lashley and Petty Officer Thomas Crean of the Royal Navy were awarded them for gallant service during the late Captain R. F. Scott's Antarctic Expedition.

23. STANHOPE GOLD MEDAL.—The Stanhope Gold Medal is awarded by the Royal Humane Society for the bravest deed of life saving of the year, either ashore or afloat. It is not awarded for bravery in saving life in fires, as cases of this kind are dealt with by another

23.

Society. The medal bears on the obverse a boy blowing an extinguished torch, in the hope, as expressed by the motto round the top circumference, " Lateat Scintillula Forsan "—" Peradventure a little spark may yet lie hid." Under the figure of the boy is the following inscription abbreviated : " Societas Londini in resuscitationem intermortuorum instituta, MDCCLXXIV "—" The (Royal Humane) Society, established in London for the recovery of persons in a state of suspended animation, 1774." The reverse shows a Civic Wreath, which was the Roman reward for saving life, while the inscription round it, " Hoc pretium; cive servato tulit "—" He has obtained this reward for

saving the life of a citizen "—expresses the merit which obtains this honour from the Society. Inside the wreath is the inscription, abbreviated, " Vitam ob servatam dono dedit societas regia humana " —" The Royal Humane Society presented this gift for saving life." There is another reverse, with the Civic Wreath only, which is used when the medal is presented to persons who have endeavoured to save the lives of others, at the risk of their own, but without success. The inscription reads, " Vita periculo exposita dono dedit societas regia humana "—" The Royal Humane Society presented this to ——. his life having been exposed to danger." The Stanhope Gold Medal is worn on the right breast, and is suspended from its ribbon by means of a straight gold clasp bearing the words, " Stanhope Medal."

24. ROYAL HUMANE SOCIETY'S MEDALS. —Besides the Stanhope Medal, the Royal Humane Society also awards silver and bronze medals for rescues, or attempted rescues, from drowning, dangerous cliffs, mines, where a fall of roof has occurred, or from suffocation by foul gas in mines, etc., provided that such cases are reported to the Society within two months of their occurrence. The Royal Humane Society's Medals are highly prized, and are eagerly sought after, and the silver medal is awarded for a more gallant deed than a bronze one. Bars may be awarded for any subsequent acts of bravery in saving, or attempting to save, life.

24.

The medals themselves are similar in design to the Stanhope Medal, already described, and are worn on the right breast, suspended from a dark blue ribbon by means of a silver scroll clasp. If the Stanhope Medal is subsequently awarded for a deed which has already been recognised by the Society by the bestowal of a silver medal, the former is worn in place of the silver medal, not in addition to it.

24.

25. BOARD OF TRADE MEDALS FOR SAVING LIFE.—The obverse of these medals bears the head of the Sovereign, with the legend " Awarded by the Board of Trade for gallantry in saving life," and the Royal cypher. The reverse shows the figure of a man holding on to a spar in the sea, and signalling to a lifeboat in the distance ; a man supporting a rescued seaman, and a woman and child seated on a rock. The medals, awarded in silver or bronze according to circumstances, are worn after war medals on the left breast, and are suspended from their ribbons by means of ornamental scroll clasps. They are given not so much for individual gallantry in saving life, for which the Albert, Stanhope, and Royal Humane Society's medals are particularly applicable, as for collective cases of heroism.

26. MEDAL OF THE ROYAL NATIONAL LIFEBOAT INSTITUTION FOR THE PRESERVATION OF LIFE FROM SHIPWRECK.—Gold and silver medals are voted by the Committee of Management of the Royal National Lifeboat Institution to "persons whose humane and intrepid exertions in saving life from shipwreck on our coasts, etc., are deemed sufficiently conspicuous to merit those honourable distinctions." The design of the medal is shown in the illustration, and bars may be awarded for subsequent acts.

26a. FOREIGN OFFICE MEDALS FOR SAVING LIFE.—Awarded by the Board of Trade, through the Foreign Office, to foreigners only. The medals are four in number, each having on the obverse the head of the reigning sovereign with the usual titular legend. The reverse bears the words PRESENTED BY (in the case of No. 3, FROM) THE BRITISH GOVERNMENT, within a wreath of oak leaves surmounted by a crown, with legend as follows: 1. For Saving the Life of a British Subject. 2. For Saving the Lives of British Subjects. 3. For Gallantry and Humanity. 4. For Assisting a British Vessel in Distress. The medals are given in gold to officers and in silver to men. They are small, the size of a half-crown piece, and are suspended by a scroll clasp from a plain crimson ribbon.

26.

27. EDWARD MEDAL. 1907.—This medal was established in 1907, for distinguishing heroic acts performed by miners and quarrymen who endanger their own lives in saving, or endeavouring to save, the lives of others from perils in mines or quarries within the King's

Dominions. In 1909 the award of the medal was extended to British subjects who, in the course of industrial employment, endanger their own lives in saving, or endeavouring to save, the lives of others from perils incurred in connection with such industrial employment.

There are two classes of the medal, the 1st being silver and the 2nd bronze, and both have swivel rings at the top through which the ribbon passes. The obverse of all the medals bears the royal effigy, with the usual titular legend. The design on the reverse of the miners' and quarrymen's medal, designed by Mr. Reynolds Stephens, shows a miner rescuing a stricken comrade and bears the words "For Courage." The reverse of the first industrial medal of 1909 showed a man holding up a beam which is about to fall on a fellow workman; but in 1911 this was replaced by one showing a classical female figure holding a wreath, the words "For Courage," with a suggestion of a manufacturing town in the background.

The cost of these medals is not provided from Imperial Funds, but from the income of a capital sum subscribed by a few gentlemen of position interested in the subject. Whenever possible the medals are presented by His Majesty in person.

28. THE KING'S POLICE MEDAL. 1909.—This medal was established in 1909 and is awarded to officers of Police or Fire Brigades in respect of one of the following qualifications:—(1) Conspicuous gallantry in saving life and property, or in preventing crime or arresting criminals; the risks incurred to be estimated with due regard to the obligations and duties of the officers concerned. (2) A specially distinguished record in administrative or detective service. (3) Success in organising Police Forces or Fire Brigades or Departments, or in maintaining their organisation under special difficulties. (4) Special services in dealing with serious or widespread outbreaks of crime or public disorder, or of fire. (5) Valuable political and secret services. (6) Special services to Royalty and Heads of States. (7) Prolonged service; but only when distinguished by very exceptional ability and merit. The number of medals is limited to 120 in any one year; 40 for the United Kingdom, 30 for H.M.'s Dominions beyond the Seas, and 50 for services in India. The medal, which is of silver and hangs from its ribbon by means of a swivel ring, bears on the obverse the effigy of the reigning Sovereign with the usual legend. The reverse shows the armed figure of a watchman leaning on a sword and bearing a shield on which is inscribed "To guard my people." In the background is a fortified city.*

29

29. MEDALS OF THE SOCIETY FOR THE PROTECTION OF LIFE FROM FIRE.—Medals, certificates, watches, and money awards are granted by the Trustees of the Society to those who display gallantry in saving life at fires. The medals, which are granted comparatively rarely, are given in silver or bronze, according to the merit of the deed, and are worn on the right breast—with other life-saving

---

* In October, 1916, the ribbon of the King's Police Medal was altered from dark blue with a narrow silver (white) stripe on either side, to dark blue with a narrow silver stripe on either side and a similar silver stripe in the centre.

medals—attached to a scarlet ribbon. One side of the medal bears two branches of oak encircling the inscription : " DUTY AND HONOR," with, round the circumference, the words " The Society for the Protection of Life from Fire," and, below, the date, " 1843." On the other side is a group of figures representing a rescue from fire.

30. QUEEN VICTORIA'S JUBILEE AND DIAMOND JUBILEE MEDALS. 1887 and 1897.—The medal has on one side the bust of Queen Victoria with the legend, " Victoria D.G. Regina et Imperatrix F.D.," and on the other, the inscription, " In commemoration of the 50th year of the Reign of Queen Victoria, June 21st 1887." The inscription is surmounted by a crown, and is encircled by a wreath of roses, thistles, and shamrock. The medal was struck in gold, silver, and bronze. The 1897 medal is the same, but the wording on the reverse has " 60th " instead of " 50th," and " June 20th 1897 " instead of the other date. On the occasion of the Queen's Jubilee in 1887, and the Diamond Jubilee in 1897, these medals were bestowed upon members of the Royal Family and the royal guests ; upon members of the Royal household, ladies, gentlemen, and servants ; upon the officers commanding the various guards of honour along the route of the Royal processions ; and officers who commanded ships present at the naval reviews at Spithead. It was also awarded to certain other officers and officials

30.

who took part in any Jubilee ceremonial at which the Queen was present. It was given in bronze to certain of the soldiers and sailors who took part in the processions through London, and who were serving on board the men-of-war when the fleets were reviewed by the Queen. Those who had already received the 1887 decoration were awarded a bar, dated " 1897 " on the occasion of the Diamond Jubilee. The ribbon passes through a ring in the top of the medal, and is worn by ladies attached to a bow of the ribbon.

31. QUEEN VICTORIA'S POLICE MEDALS FOR THE JUBILEE AND DIAMOND JUBILEE OF 1887 AND 1897.—This medal, which is suspended by a plain clasp, bears on one side, the head of Queen Victoria. On the other there is an oak wreath and a crown with, inside, the words, " Jubilee of Her Majesty Queen Victoria," and outside, " City of London Police," or " Metropolitan Police," as the case may be. Below is the date " 1887," or " 1897," with a heraldic rose on either side. The medals were given in silver or bronze —according to rank—to all members of the police forces who were on duty in London during the Jubilee processions of 1887 and 1897. A bronze medal, hung from the same ribbon, was awarded to the Dublin Metropolitan Police and men of the Royal Irish Constabulary who were on duty during the Royal visit in 1900. The obverse bears the head of the Queen with the usual legend, and the reverse a figure of Hibernia and a view of Kingstown Harbour, with the date "1900."

32. KING EDWARD VII.'S CORONATION MEDALS. 1902. —This medal bears on the obverse the busts of King Edward and Queen

Alexandra side by side, crowned, and facing to the right. On the other side it has the Royal cypher " E.R. VII." with a crown above it, and the date " June 26th 1902." It is oval with a raised ornamental rim, is rather smaller than ordinary war medals, and is surmounted by a crown and a ring through which the ribbon passes. The medal, in silver and bronze, was awarded in much the same way as Queen Victoria's Jubilee medals. Amongst other recipients it was given in bronze to one seaman or marine of " very good " character on board each of the ships present at the naval review at Spithead on August 16th, 1902. A rather similar medal was bestowed upon provincial mayors and others who took part in the Coronation ceremony. It has a raised rim, has no crown between the ring and the medal, is round, not oval. It is suspended from a ribbon with a narrow white stripe down the centre, a blue stripe on either side of the white, and wide scarlet edges.

33. KING EDWARD'S POLICE CORONATION MEDALS. 1902.—This medal has on the obverse the head of King Edward, with the usual wording. On the reverse is the inscription " Coronation of His Majesty King Edward VII., 1902," and the words " Metropolitan Police." Below, a crown with a branch of oak with laurel on either side. It was issued in silver or bronze, according to rank, to all members of the police forces who were on duty during the Coronation procession through London. The same medal, with the words " St. John's Ambulance Brigade," or " Metropolitan Fire Brigade," on the reverse, was given to members of the ambulance corps and fire brigades on duty on the same occasion.

34. KING EDWARD'S DELHI DURBAR MEDAL. 1903.— On one side there is the bust of King Edward with the words " Edward VII., Delhi Durbar, 1903." On the reverse there is a native inscription which reads, " By the favour of the Lord of Dominion, Edward the Seventh, Emperor of India." This medal was awarded in gold, silver, or bronze, according to the rank of the recipient. It was given to officers, civil officials, prominent civilians, and to certain of the soldiers and others who took a prominent part in the Durbar. The medal is suspended by means of a ring.

35. KING EDWARD'S MEDAL. IRELAND. 1903.—This medal bears on one side the bust of the King with the usual wording. On the other appears a figure of Hibernia, with a view of the Royal yacht entering Kingstown harbour. At the feet of the figure is a harp, rose, and shamrock. The date " 1903 " appears below. Given in silver and bronze on the occasion of King Edward's visit to Ireland in 1903. Most of the recipients were members of the police forces.

36. KING GEORGE V.'S CORONATION MEDAL. 1911.—This medal, which is suspended from its ribbon by means of a ring, bears on one side the busts of King George and Queen Mary, side by side, facing left. On the other side appears the

36.

Royal cypher, "G.R.v.," surmounted by an Imperial crown, with the date " 22 June 1911 " below. A beaded circle runs round the circumference. The medal, which was struck in silver only, was awarded during the Coronation festivities in 1911, in much the same way as Queen Victoria's Jubilee medals, and that for King Edward's Coronation. King George's medal for the Delhi Durbar of 1911 is suspended from the same ribbon, but is somewhat larger and of a different design. Both these medals were awarded to ladies, and are worn by them on the left shoulder, attached to a bow of the ribbon.

37. KING GEORGE V.'S POLICE CORONATION MEDAL. 1911.—Awarded to members of the police forces, ambulance brigades, and fire brigades in the same way as King Edward's Police Coronation Medal. It was given in silver.

38. KING'S VISIT COMMEMORATION MEDAL. IRELAND. 1911.—Awarded to prominent officials in Ireland, and to members of the Irish Police Forces in much the same way as King Edward's medal, 1903, No. 35.

39. UNION OF SOUTH AFRICA COMMEMORATION MEDAL. 1910.—This silver medal was awarded to those officials and civilians, and to certain naval and military officers and men, who took a prominent part in the ceremonies in connection with the union of the various South African states and provinces by H.R.H. the Duke of Connaught in 1910. Also to certain officers of H.M.S. *Balmoral Castle*, which vessel—a Union Castle liner—was specially commissioned as a man-of-war to convey His Royal Highness to the Cape of Good Hope. The obverse bears the effigy of King George with the usual legend, and the reverse a figure at an anvil welding together the links of a chain, typical of the uniting of the various South African territories into one. The medal, which is suspended from its ribbon by means of a ring, takes precedence after war medals and those for long service and good conduct.

40. THE KAISAR-I-HIND MEDAL.— This medal was instituted in May, 1900, and may be given to any person, irrespective of race, occupation, position, or sex, who shall have distinguished himself, or herself, by important or useful service in the advancement of the public interest in India. There are two classes, the first being bestowed by the Sovereign, and the second by the Governor General in India. The decoration consists of an oval badge in gold for the 1st Class, and in silver for the 2nd. The obverse bears the Imperial cypher in the centre, and the reverse the words "Kaisar-i-Hind, for public service in India." The medal, when awarded to ladies, is worn attached to the left shoulder by a bow of the ribbon, and when given to men is suspended from the left breast in the usual manner.

40.

41. BADGE OF THE ORDER OF THE LEAGUE OF MERCY.—

The Badge of this Order consists of a red cross surmounted by the badge of the Heir-Apparent— a plume of ostrich feathers enfiled by a coronet,— and having in the centre a group of figures representing " Charity." Appointments to the Order are approved and sanctioned by His Majesty on the recommendation of the Grand President of the League of Mercy, as a reward for distinguished personal service on behalf of the League in assisting the support of hospitals, or in connection with the relief of suffering, poverty, or distress. Ladies or gentlemen who have rendered gratuitously the required services to the League for five years at least, are eligible for the Order.

41.

42. ST. JOHN OF JERUSALEM SERVICE MEDAL.—This medal, in silver, is awarded for conspicuous services to the Order of St. John of Jerusalem in England and its departments. It has on the obverse the effigy of the Sovereign surrounded by the usual legend. In the centre of the reverse is a small circle containing the Royal arms surrounded by the garter and motto. At the top, bottom, right, and left of this are four small circles containing an Imperial Crown, the Prince of Wales' feathers, and the badges of the Order. Between the circles are sprigs of St. John's Wort. Round the circumference is the inscription, " Magnus Prioratus Ordinis Hospitalis Sancti Johannis Jerusalem in Anglia," in old English lettering. The medal hangs from its ribbon by means of a ring, and is worn on the left breast.

43. MEDAL FOR SOUTH AFRICA, 1899–1902, GIVEN TO MEMBERS OF ST. JOHN OF JERUSALEM AMBULANCE BRIGADES.—This medal, which is of bronze, bears on one side the bust of King Edward, with the usual legend, and on the other the arms of the Order of Saint John of Jerusalem, with the words, " South Africa 1899–1902 " above, and the motto, " Pro fide : pro utilitate : hominum " on a scroll below. The medal hangs from its black, white-edged, ribbon by a straight clasp, and it was awarded to members of the St. John of Jerusalem Ambulance Brigades who served in South Africa during the war, also to those who had to do with the despatch of medical comforts, stores, etc.

44. ARCTIC AND ANTARCTIC MEDALS.—Various medals have been issued between 1857 and the present time for the expeditions of voyage and discovery in the Arctic and Antarctic Seas. The first, established in 1857, was awarded to all persons of every rank and class who had been engaged in the various expeditions to the Arctic between the years 1818 and 1855. The medal, which is octagonal, bears on the obverse the head of Queen Victoria with the usual legend. The reverse shows a ship blocked in the ice with icebergs to right and left, and a sledge party in the foreground. Above appear the words " For Arctic Discoveries," and below the dates " 1818–1855." At the top of the medal is a five-pointed star, surmounted by a ring, and the white watered ribbon, one and a half inches wide, passes through the latter. The next medal was issued in 1876, to all persons who served on

board H.M. ships *Alert* and *Discovery*, during the Arctic Expedition of
1875–76, and to the officers and crew of the yacht *Pandora*, during her
voyage in the Arctic regions, June–November, 1876.
The medal is circular, and bears on one side the head
of Queen Victoria, with the usual legend and date,
"1876." The reverse shows a ship in the ice-pack,
with clouds in the sky above the vessel. It hangs
from a straight silver clasp, and is worn with a white
unwatered ribbon, one and a quarter inches wide.
Another medal was issued by King Edward in 1904
to the men who took part in the late Captain R. F.
Scott's first Antarctic expedition in the *Discovery*,
1901–1904. The medal is octagonal, and has on the
obverse the effigy of King Edward in naval uniform,
with the legend "Edwardus VII Rex Imperator,"
and on the reverse the *Discovery* in winter quarters,
with, in the foreground, a sledge dragged by men on
skis, and in the background a representation of
Mount Erebus. The ribbon is pure white and is one
and a quarter inches wide, and the medal hangs by
means of a scroll clasp. All those serving on board
the *Discovery* received the medal in silver, with a bar

44.

inscribed, "ANTARCTIC 1902–1904," while the officers
and men of the relief ships *Morning* and *Terra Nova* were awarded
the medal in bronze without the clasp. This medal, with the head of
the reigning Sovereign, is now used for Arctic and Antarctic explora-
tion generally, and, with appropriate bars, has been given for all
subsequent expeditions, including the one in which the intrepid
Captain Robert Falcon Scott lost his life. Arctic and Antarctic medals,
on account of the small number of men who receive them, are very
rare indeed.

45. MEDAL FOR THE BEST SHOT IN THE BRITISH ARMY.
1870.—This medal has on one side the head of Queen Victoria, with the
usual inscription, and on the other a figure of Fame standing on a dais.
She has a horn in her left hand, and with her right is crowning a kneeling
warrior with a wreath of laurel. The warrior is armed with a bow,
and holds a shield pierced by three arrows. The medal was instituted
in 1869, and was awarded each year, with a gratuity of £20, to the
best rifle shot in the British Army. It was issued in bronze until 1872,
and then in silver, and was worn on the right breast. It became obsolete
in 1883, and as only thirteen of the medals were awarded, specimens
are very rare indeed. A somewhat similar medal, with the same ribbon,
was at one time presented to the best rifle shot in the Indian Army.

46. NAVAL GOOD SHOOTING MEDAL. 1903.—This medal,
which is suspended by a plain clasp, bears the effigy of the reigning
Sovereign in naval uniform on one side, with the usual inscription.
On the reverse appears a figure of Neptune turned towards the right.
He grasps thunderbolts in each hand, and the right arm is drawn
back in the act of throwing them. In the background is the prow
of a Roman trireme drawn by three sea-horses. Above there is a
trident, with the wording "Amat Victoria curam." This medal was
authorised by King Edward in August, 1903, and is now given yearly

to seamen who attain a certain very high percentage of hits with each

40.

type of gun during the annual target practice carried out by the Fleet. The medal is first awarded without a bar, but if a man qualifies for it again, he receives a bar on which appears the name of his ship, the calibre or denomination of the gun with which he fired, and the year. The Naval Good Shooting Medal is rare, and is most highly sought after.

47. TRANSPORT MEDAL.—This medal was instituted by King Edward in 1903, and was first awarded to certain officers of the specially chartered transports who had been employed in carrying troops during the South African War, 1899–1902,

and during the China campaign of 1900. A similar medal will probably

47.

be granted at the conclusion of the present war, for it was officially stated that the medal would be granted "in future wars to the officers of the Mercantile Marine serving in the transports" whenever a medal was issued to the troops taking part in the campaign. The medal bears on the obverse the bust of King Edward in naval uniform with the usual legend. The reverse shows a map of the Southern Hemisphere with a liner steaming through the ocean. Below is the inscription, " Ob Patriam Militibus per Mare transvecti adjutam." The medal hangs from its ribbon by a straight silver clasp, and bars inscribed, "CHINA 1900," or

" S. AFRICA 1899–1902," have already been issued.

48. NAVAL GENERAL SERVICE MEDAL. 1793–1840.—One side of this medal bears the diademed head of Queen Victoria, the

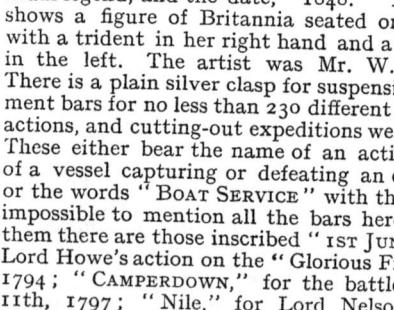

48.

usual legend, and the date, " 1848." The other side shows a figure of Britannia seated on a sea-horse, with a trident in her right hand and a laurel branch in the left. The artist was Mr. W. Wyon, R.A. There is a plain silver clasp for suspension. Engagement bars for no less than 230 different engagements, actions, and cutting-out expeditions were authorised. These either bear the name of an action, the name of a vessel capturing or defeating an enemy's ship, or the words " BOAT SERVICE " with the date. It is impossible to mention all the bars here, but among them there are those inscribed " 1ST JUNE, 1794," for Lord Howe's action on the " Glorious First of June," 1794 ; " CAMPERDOWN," for the battle of October 11th, 1797 ; " Nile," for Lord Nelson's battle in Aboukir Bay, August 1st, 1798 ; " COPENHAGEN," April 2nd, 1801 ; " TRAFALGAR," October 21st, 1805 ; " SHANNON WITH CHESAPEAKE," June 1st, 1813 ; " NAVARINO," October 20th, 1827. The last bar issued was that inscribed " SYRIA," for the operations of November, 1840. This medal was not issued until 1848. Included in the list of recipients of the medal with the bar for

" June 1st, 1794," was Daniel Tremendous McKenzie, of H.M.S. *Tremendous*. He was officially styled as "Baby." At that time a certain proportion of the seamen were allowed to take their wives to sea with them, and "Tremendous McKenzie" was born at sea shortly before the action. Various Army officers and soldiers received the naval medal and bars, for during the wars for which it was issued troops were not infrequently embarked on board men-of-war instead of Royal Marines. Naval General Service Medals with, amongst others, bars for the following actions were issued to certain officers and men of the Army who were serving on board H.M. ships: "1ST JUNE, 1794"; "ST. VINCENT," Sept. 14th, 1797; "COPENHAGEN," April 2nd, 1801; "ST. SEBASTIAN," Aug.–Sept., 1813; "ALGIERS," Aug. 27th, 1815; "NAVARINO," Oct. 20th, 1827; "SYRIA," Nov., 1840.

49. MILITARY GENERAL SERVICE MEDAL. 1793–1814.— The obverse of this medal is the same as that of the Naval General Service medal just described. Upon the reverse appears an upright figure of Queen Victoria standing on a dais. She is crowning the kneeling figure of the Duke of Wellington with a wreath of laurel. By the side of the dais is the British lion couchant. Round the top circumference are the words "To the British Army"; "1793–1814" at the bottom. Mr. W. Wyon, R.A., was the artist. The ribbon for suspension passes through a plain clasp at the top of the medal. Twenty-nine different engagement bars were issued with this medal, and though the latter was to be bestowed for services from 1793 till 1814, it will be noticed that no bars were awarded for services before 1801, or between 1801 and 1806. The following is a list of the bars awarded: "EGYPT." This

49.

bar, for the campaign of 1801, was granted in 1850, to those soldiers who had taken part in the operations and "were still alive." "MAIDA," for the battle in Calabria of July 4th, 1806. "ROLEIA," for the engagement of August 17th, 1808, Peninsula War. "VIMIERA," for the battle of August 21st, 1808, Peninsula War. "SAHAGUN," Dec. 21st, 1808, Peninsula War. "BENEVENTE," Dec. 29th, 1808, Peninsula War. (A single bar inscribed "SAHAGUN & BENEVENTE" was given to those men who had fought in both engagements.) "CORUNNA," Jan. 16th, 1809, Peninsula War. "MARTINIQUE," Feb. 24th, 1809, West Indies. "TALAVERA," July 27th–28th, 1809, Peninsula War. "GUADALOUPE," Jan.–Feb., 1810, West Indies. "BUSACO," Sept. 27th, 1810, Peninsula War. "BARROSA," March 5th, 1811, Peninsula War. "FUENTES D'ONOR," May 5th, 1811, Peninsula War. "ALBUERA," May 16th, 1811, Peninsula War. "JAVA," Aug.–Sept., 1811. "CIUDAD ROD-RIGO," Jan. 19th, 1812, Peninsula War. "BADAJOZ," March 17th–April 6th, 1812, Peninsula War. "SALAMANCA," July 22nd, 1812, Peninsula War. "FORT DETROIT," Aug. 16th, 1812, North America. "CHATEAUGUAY," Oct. 26th, 1812, N. America. "CHRYSTLER'S FARM," Nov. 11th, 1813, N. America. "VITTORIA," June 21st, 1813, Peninsula War. "PYRENEES," July 28th–Aug. 2nd, 1813, Peninsula War. "ST. SEBASTIAN," Aug.–Sept., 1813, Peninsula War. "NIVELLE," Nov. 16th, 1813, Peninsula War. "NIVE," Dec. 9th–13th, 1813, Peninsula War. "ORTHES," Feb. 17th, 1814, Peninsula War; and

D

"TOULOUSE," April 10th, 1814, Peninsula War. A ribbon of the same colours, but only one inch wide, is now used for the D.S.O. Senior officers of the Army had previously been granted gold medals and bars for all the engagements and battles mentioned above, but no medal had been bestowed upon the junior officers or the rank and file. There was considerable feeling in the matter, and no little discussion in the Houses of Parliament, and to rectify the omission the Army General Service Medal was eventually sanctioned by Queen Victoria in 1847, and was issued the following year to all surviving officers and men who had been in any of the battles mentioned. The Duke of Richmond was almost entirely responsible for the grant of the medal, and, it may be said, the officers interested in the grant of it presented him with a piece of plate to the value of 1500 guineas. One naval officer, Lieutenant Carroll, received the Army medal and bar for

"MAIDA," while a few other officers of the Royal Navy and Royal Marines were awarded it with the "GUADALOUPE" and "JAVA" bars.

49. Ribbon 1½ inches wide. WATERLOO MEDAL. 1815.—This medal bears on the obverse the effigy of H.R.H. the Prince Regent, with the words "George P. Regent." On the reverse is a winged figure of Victory seated on a plinth, the base of which bears the word "Waterloo." Round the top circumference is the name "Wellington," and at the bottom the date "June 18th, 1815." The artist was Mr. Thomas Wyon. When issued the medal was suspended by means of a large steel ring through which the ribbon passed, but many officers and men had the ring removed and an ornamental silver bar substituted. No engagement bars were issued, as the medal bears the name of the battle. The medal was issued in 1816–17, at the suggestion

49.

of the Duke of Wellington, and besides being bestowed upon all officers and men who had been at Waterloo, was given to those who had fought at the Battle of Ligny on June 16th, and at Quatre Bras on June 17th.

49. Ribbon 1½ inches wide. FIRST BURMAH MEDAL. 1824–26. —One side of this medal shows the white elephant of Ava kneeling before a victorious British lion. In the background is a Union Jack and palm trees. Below a Persian inscription reading, "The elephant of Ava submitting to the British lion. 1826." On the obverse is shown an attacking party advancing towards a pagoda. In the foreground is the dismounted figure of Sir A. Campbell directing the operations from beneath a palm tree. A steamer in the left background. Below, in Persian, is the inscription, "The Standard of the victorious army of England in Ava." The ribbon passed through a steel ring like that of the Waterloo Medal. This medal was issued by the East India Company in 1826, to the Madras and Bengal native troops.

It was given in gold to officers, and in silver to others, and no engagement bars were issued. Naval officers and men who had served in the Irrawaddy flotilla during the campaign subsequently received the "India Medal, 1799–1826," with bar for "AVA."

50. FIRST INDIA MEDAL. 1799–1826.—On the obverse is the head of Queen Victoria with the legend "Victoria Regina." The reverse has a seated winged figure of Victory in the foreground. She holds a laurel wreath in one hand and a wreath in the other. Above appears the inscription "To the Army of India" and below the dates "1799–1826." Artist, Mr. W. Wyon, R.A. The ribbon passes through an ornamental scroll clasp at the top of the medal. This medal was the counterpart for the troops in India of the Army General Service Medal. It was issued in 1851 at the request and expense of the Hon. East India Company. Bars for the following battles were issued:
"ALLIGHUR:" storming of Allighur, Sept. 4th, 1803.
"BATTLE OF DELHI," Sept. 11th, 1803, Mahrattas
defeated by British. "ASSAYE:" Sept. 23rd, 1803,
Mahrattas defeated by Wellesley. "ASSEERGHUR:"
siege of Asseerghur, Oct. 21st, 1803. "LASWARREE,"
Nov. 1st, 1803. "ARGAUM:" battle of Argaum,
Nov. 26th, 1803. "GAWILGHUR:" siege and storm-
ing of Gawilghur, Dec. 15th, 1803. "DEFENCE OF
DELHI:" Oct. 7th–16th, 1804, besieging force of
Mahrattas defeated by British. "BATTLE OF DEIG,"
Nov. 13th, 1804. "CAPTURE OF DEIG," Dec. 23rd,
1804. "NEPAUL:" war in Nepaul, 1816. "KIR-
KEE," Nov. 1817. "POONA:" battle and capture
of Poona, Nov. 1817. "KIRKEE AND POONA:"

50.

battles of Kirkee and Poona, Nov. 1817. "SEETA-
BULDEE:" battle of Seetabuldee, Nov. and Dec. 1817. "NAGPORE:"
battle and capture of Nagpore, Nov. and Dec. 1817. "SEETABULDEE
AND NAGPORE." "MAHEIDPOOR:" battle of Maheidpoor, Dec. 21st,
1817. "CORYGAUM:" defence of Corygaum, Jan. 1st, 1818. "AVA:"
war in Ava, 1824–6. "BHURTPOOR:" siege and storming of Bhurtpoor,
Jan. 1826.

51. MEDAL FOR THE CAPTURE OF GHUZNEE. JULY
1839.—This medal has on one side a representation of the gateway of
the fortress of Ghuznee, with the word "Ghuznee" in a scroll below.
On the other side are two branches of laurel with, inside them, a mural
crown. Above, "23rd July," below, "1839." The ribbon passes
through a plain clasp at the top of the medal. No engagement bars
were issued. This medal was originally to have been conferred by the
Shah Shoojah-ool-Moolk on the troops engaged in the capture of
Ghuznee. The Shah Shoojah died, however, before the medal was
issued, and it was subsequently bestowed in 1842 in the name of the
Indian Government. The ribbon was originally intended to be half
green and half yellow, instead of crimson and green. How the change
came to be made is not known.

52. JELLALABAD MEDAL. 1842.—On one side is the head of
Queen Victoria with the legend "Victoria Vindex." On the other side
is a winged figure of Victory flying over the fortress of Jellalabad.
She carries a Union Jack in one hand and a laurel wreath in the other.
Above is "Jellalabad. VII April," and below the year, "MDCCCXLII."
The artist was Mr. William Wyon. The medal was hung from its
ribbon by means of a plain german-silver clasp, and no engagement
bars were issued. A Jellalabad medal was first issued in December,

1842, to the European and native troops who defended the fortress. It did not bear the effigy of Queen Victoria, and was of a very rough design, and the medal described above was intended to supersede it. The men, however, preferred the original medal first issued, and comparatively few of the later ones were applied for in exchange. This ribbon is supposed to represent an Eastern sky at sunrise : pink merging into yellow, and yellow into blue. Its colouring is most striking, and the ribbon was revived for the " Kabul to Kandahar Bronze Star " of 1880.

52. CANDAHAR, GHUZNEE, AND CABUL MEDALS. 1842.—
The obverse of these medals bear the diademed head of Queen Victoria

52.

with the wording " Victoria Vindex." There are four different reverses : (1) A crown, the word " Candahar," and the date, " 1842," inside a wreath of laurel. (2) A crown, the words " Ghuznee " and " Cabul," each in a laurel wreath, with " 1842 " below. (3) The same as No. 1, but with the names " Candahar," " Ghuznee," and " Cabul." (4) The same as No. 1, but with the name " Cabul " only. The medals are suspended from their ribbons by means of plain steel clasps, and were designed by Mr. William Wyon, R.A. They were given for the operations in Afghanistan in 1842, and were issued by the Indian Government. The specimen inscribed " Candahar " was awarded to those officers and men who had been in action in the vicinity of that place. No. 2 (Ghuznee. Cabul) was given to those who were present at the operations resulting in the capture of Ghuznee and occupation of Cabul ; while No. 3 was bestowed on those entitled to both the above. No. 4 was awarded to those officers and men who were present at the operations culminating in the occupation of Cabul.

52. MEDAL FOR THE DEFENCE OF KELAT-I-GHILZIE. 1842.—This medal was specially struck for the heroic defence of the fort of Kelat-i-Ghilzie, May, 1842. The garrison consisted of 950 men, and of these one irregular regiment of Shah Shooja's force, in recognition of its gallant conduct during the siege, was specially brought to the strength of the Bengal Army under the name of the " Regiment of Kelat-i-Ghilzie." Its regimental colours were composed of the three colours of the military medal ribbon of India, red, yellow, and blue, arranged horizontally as in the Dutch flag. The Kelat-i-Ghilzie medal has on one side a shield bearing the word " Kelat-i-Ghilzie," surmounted by a mural crown and encircled by branches of laurel. On the reverse appears a trophy of arms, with, below it, a tablet with the word " INVICTA " and the date " MDCCCXLII." The medal has a steel clasp for suspension.

52. SINDE MEDAL. 1843.—This medal was awarded for Sir Charles Napier's conquest of Sinde. It bears on one side the head of Queen Victoria, with the legend " Victoria Regina." There are three different reverses : (1) A laurel wreath surrounding a crown, the word " MEEANEE," and the date, " 1843." (2) The same, but with the word " HYDERABAD " instead of " MEEANEE." (3) The same, but with " HYDERABAD " in addition to " MEEANEE." The artist was Mr. W. Wyon, R.A., and the medal is provided with a plain steel clasp for suspension. The action at Meeanee was fought on February 17th, 1843, and that at Hyderabad on March 24th the same year. The appropriate medals were awarded to the officers and men who had been in one or both of the battles. The officers and crews of the Hon. East India Company's vessels *Comet*, *Planet*, *Meteor*, and *Satellite*, also received it, as these four ships formed the flotilla which took part in the campaign. The cost of these medals was borne by the Home Government, this being the only case on record where medals for Indian service were not paid for by the Indian Government.

52. STARS FOR GWALIOR CAMPAIGN.   1843.—Stars made of bronze from guns captured at the Battles of Maharajpoor and Punniar during the Gwalior campaign of 1843, were presented by the Government of India to all officers and men present at those engagements. They consist of six-pointed bronze stars two inches in diameter with small silver stars in the centre. Round the centre of the silver stars are the names and year, " MAHARAJPOOR. 1843," or " PUNNIAR. 1843," as the case may be, and in the centre itself the date, " Dec. 29th." The back of the stars are quite plain. When first issued these decorations were fitted with hooks and were intended to be worn on the breast of the coat like the stars of Orders of Knighthood. Subsequently, however, the recipients fitted suspension clasps or rings, according to their individual fancies, and wore them as medals with the then usual Indian ribbon.

52.

53. 1½ inches wide. CHINA MEDAL.   1842.—This medal was given to the men of the Navy and Army who had taken part in the following operations in China :—In the Canton River, 1841. At Chusan in 1841 and 1842. At Amoy, Ningpo, Chinpae, Tsekee, Chapoo ; in the Yang-tse-kiang ; in the Woosung River ; and in the assault upon Ching-Kiang-Foo. No engagement bars were issued. The medal bears on one side the effigy of Queen Victoria with the usual legend, and on the other a palm tree, an oval shield with the Royal arms, and a trophy of weapons. Round the top circumference is the inscription, " Armis exposcere pacem," and at the bottom the word " China," and the date " 1842." A plain german-silver clasp was provided for suspension. The artist was Mr. William Wyon, R.A. The crimson in this ribbon is said to represent the heraldic colour of Great Britain, and the yellow the Imperial colour of China.

53.

54. MEDAL FOR SUTLEJ CAMPAIGN.   (SIKH WAR.) 1845–46.—The obverse of this medal has the effigy of Queen Victoria and the usual wording. Upon the reverse appears a figure of Victory holding out a laurel wreath in her right hand. In her left is a palm branch, and at her feet a pile of captured weapons. The words " Army

of the Sutlej " round the top circumference, and at the bottom the name and date of the battle for which the medal was struck. The medal was provided with an ornamental scroll clasp for suspension from its ribbon. The artist was Mr. William Wyon, R.A. Medals with the following battles inscribed on the reverse were issued. " MOODKEE 1845," " FEROZESHUHUR 1845," " ALIWAL 1846," " SOBRAON 1846." For his first engagement a soldier received the medal with the corresponding inscription, and if he subsequently took part in another he was given an engagement bar bearing the name of the second. Similarly with second and third bars for his third and fourth engagements. This was the first instance of bars being granted with any Indian medal, the first Indian Medal, 1799–1826, with bars for battles previous to 1845, not being authorised until 1849.

54.

55. NEW ZEALAND MEDAL. 1845–66.— The obverse bears the diademed head of Queen Victoria wearing a veil, with the legend, " Victoria D.G. Britt. Reg. F.D." The reverse has a wreath of laurel, inside of which appear the dates of service of the recipient. The words "New Zealand" appear above, and " Virtutis Honor " below. The medal hangs from its ribbon by an embossed silver clasp. The New Zealand medal was not authorised until 1869, and was then issued to the officers and men of the Navy and Army for services against the Maoris between 1845 and 1847, and again for the operations carried out from 1860 to 1866. No engagement bars were given, but the medal bears on the obverse the dates between which the recipients served.

55.

56. PUNJAB MEDAL. 1848–49.—The obverse has the effigy of Queen Victoria with the usual wording. On the reverse is a party of Sikhs laying down their arms to General Sir Walter Raleigh Gilbert, who appears on horseback. To the right is a file of British troops with colours flying, and in the background a hill surmounted by palm trees. " To the Army of the Punjab " round the top ; " MDCCCXLIX " at the bottom. The medal hangs from an ornamental scroll clasp. This decoration was given to the officers and men of the Navy and Army for the war which ended in the annexation of the Punjab. Three engagement bars were issued, inscribed respectively " MOOLTAN," " CHILIANWALA," and " GOOJERAT." The first was awarded for the

56.

operations before Mooltan, Dec. 27th, 1848, to Jan. 21st, 1849; the second, for the Battle of Chilianwala, Jan. 13th, 1849: and the third, for the Battle of Goojerat, Feb. 21st, 1849. The bars were awarded according as to whether the recipient had been in one, or more, battles, but a large number of medals were given without them.

57. INDIA GENERAL SERVICE MEDAL. 1854.—This medal has on the obverse the usual head of Queen Victoria with the customary legend. The reverse shows a winged figure of Victory crowning a seated warrior with a wreath of laurel. Below a lotus flower and leaves, emblematic of the East. An ornamental scroll clasp is provided for suspension. This medal was first issued in 1854, to "commemorate the services rendered against the Burmese in 1852–53." It was used subsequently, however, for many campaigns and expeditions against the native tribes, and was not finally discontinued until 1895. It was Lord Dalhousie, the Governor General of India, who, in 1852, first suggested that a general service medal for India should be adopted, and that the medal, with appropriate bars, should be given for all suc-

57.

ceeding campaigns in India. Medals had recently become very numerous, and the idea was to limit their number. The medal was issued for a large number of small wars and expeditions, with the following bars: "PEGU," "PERSIA," "NORTH-WEST FRONTIER," "UMBEYLA," "BHOOTAN," "LOOSHAI," "PERAK," "JOWAKI 1877–8," "NAGA 1879–80," "BURMA 1885–7," "SIKKIM 1888," "HAZARA 1888," "BURMA 1887–9," "CHIN-LUSHAI 1889–90," "SAMANA 1891," "HAZARA 1891," "N.E. FRONTIER 1891," "HUNZA 1891," "BURMA 1889–92," "LUSHAI 1889–92," "CHIN HILLS 1892–93," "KACHIN HILLS 1892–93," "WAZIRISTAN 1894–5."

58. MEDALS FOR SOUTH AFRICA. 1834–5, 1846–7, 1850–53, 1877–9.—A medal for the campaigns against the Kaffirs of 1834–5, 1846–7, and 1850–3, was issued in 1854. They all bore the date "1853." The same medal, with bars inscribed "1877–8," "1878," "1878–9," "1879," and "1877–8–9," was again given for the campaigns of 1877–79 against the Galeka, Gaika, Zulu, and other Kaffir tribes, the principle being that the date or dates on the bar covered all the operations in which the recipients were engaged. The medal without bars was also given to the troops employed in Natal during the Zulu War. The obverse of all the medals is the same, and bears the diademed head of Queen Victoria with the customary inscription. The reverse shows a British lion crouching behind a bush with the words "South Africa" above. The medal issued in 1854 has the date

58.

"1853" below the lion, but in the "1877–9" specimen the date is replaced by a Zulu shield, and assegais. They both have an ornamental scroll clasp for suspension.

N.B.—The ribbon for the earlier medals was of a paler shade of orange than that shown in No. 58, which is the ribbon for the medal of the 1877–9 campaign.

59. CRIMEA MEDAL. 1854–6.—The obverse of this medal bears the head of Queen Victoria, the usual wording, and the date "1854."

59.

The reverse shows a flying figure of Victory crowning with a laurel wreath a Roman warrior armed with a shield and sword. The word "Crimea" is inscribed vertically on the left. The medal is hung from its ribbon by an ornamental foliated clasp, and its issue, with bars inscribed, "INKERMANN" and "ALMA" for those two battles, was authorised in December, 1854, while the Crimean War was yet in progress. Subsequent orders, however, authorised additional bars being granted for "BALAKLAVA" and "SEBASTOPOL," while another, "AZOFF," was awarded to the Navy for the operations in the Sea of Azoff. Medals with the "Balaclava" bar awarded to the 17th Lancers, 13th Light Dragoons, 11th Hussars, 4th Light Dragoons, and the 8th Hussars, are most highly prized by collectors on account of the historic charge of the Light Brigade. The bars for the Crimean medal are in the form of oak leaves, with the name of the engagement in raised letters. They are most unusual and artistic. The British medal was given to a limited number of French soldiers who fought as our Allies during the campaign.

60. BALTIC MEDAL. 1854–55.—The Baltic medal bears the usual head of Queen Victoria and legend. On the reverse is a seated figure of Britannia holding a trident, with a representation of the fortress of Bomarsund and Fort Sveaborg in the background. The word "Baltic" appears at the top, and at the bottom the dates "1854–1855." The medal hangs from an ornamental scroll clasp, and no engagement bars were issued. It was issued to the officers and men serving on board H.M. ships which were in the Baltic in the years 1854 and 1855, and was also given to two officers and ninety men of the Sappers and Miners who served on board the Flagship.

60.

61. INDIAN MUTINY MEDAL. 1857–58.—This has the usual Queen's head and legend on the obverse. On the reverse is a standing figure of Britannia with a shield. Her right hand is outstretched with a wreath of laurel. The British lion appears in the background. The word "India" appears round the top circumference, and below the dates "1857–58." The artist responsible for the reverse was Mr. Leonard Wyon. The medal is suspended from its ribbon by an ornamental clasp. The decoration was awarded to the British troops employed in the Indian Mutiny, and, amongst others, was given to the officers and men of H.M.S. *Pearl* and *Shannon*, and to the crews of the Hon. East India Company's vessels *Calcutta* and *Sans Pareil*. It was the last medal given by the Hon. East India Company in the name of the British Government. The following bars were issued: "DELHI." Granted to those employed in the operations against, and at the assault of, Delhi. May 30th to Sept. 14th, 1857. "DEFENCE OF LUCKNOW." Granted to all those who formed part of the original garrison under Major-General Sir John Inglis; and to those who succoured them, and continued the defence under Major-Generals Havelock and Outram, until relieved by Lord Clyde. June 29th–Nov. 17th, 1857. "RELIEF OF LUCKNOW." Granted to the troops engaged in the operations against Lucknow, under the immediate command of Lord Clyde. Nov. 1857. "LUCKNOW." Granted to those engaged in the operations against Lucknow, under the immediate command of Lord Clyde. Nov. 1857 and March, 1858. "CENTRAL INDIA." Granted to the troops employed in the operations against Jhansi, Calpee, and Gwalior, and to those employed in Central India. Jan.–June, 1858.

61.

63. CHINA MEDAL. 1857–60.—This medal is of exactly the same design as that given for China, 1842, except that the date " 1842 " on the reverse is omitted. It is suspended from its ribbon by an ornamental clasp. It was authorised in 1861, and was first issued with a ribbon of five stripes: blue, yellow, red, white, and green, No. **62.** Eventually, however, it was replaced by the crimson ribbon with yellow edges shown in No. 63. The crimson was much darker than that in the 1842 ribbon. The decoration was given to officers and men of both the Navy and Army, and the following bars were issued: "CHINA, 1842." To those entitled to the new medal who were already in possession of the one for 1842. "CANTON, 1857." To those who were employed in the operations against that city. "TAKU FORTS, 1858." To those present at the capture, 23rd May, 1858. "TAKU FORTS, 1860." To those employed in the capture of the forts, Aug. 21st, 1860. "PEKIN, 1860." To those employed in the operations resulting in the capture of Pekin, Oct. 1860. "FATSHAN, 1857." To those naval officers and men present at the battle.

64. CANADA GENERAL SERVICE MEDAL. 1866–70.—The issue of this medal, which was presented by the Canadian Government was not authorised until January, 1899. It was given to soldiers of the British Army, and to those of the Canadian Militia, who were employed on active service during the Fenian Raids of 1866 and 1870, and the Red River expedition of 1870. Three bars were issued, inscribed respectively: "FENIAN RAID, 1866," "FENIAN RAID, 1870," and "RED RIVER, 1870." The medal bears on one side the effigy of Queen Victoria, crowned and veiled, with the legend "Victoria Regina et Imperatrix," and on the

64.

other, the Canadian flag surrounded by a wreath of maple. The word "CANADA" appears at the top, and the medal hangs from a straight clasp.

65. ABYSSINIAN MEDAL. 1867–68.—The obverse of this medal has a small bust of Queen Victoria within a beaded circle. The circle forms the centre of a nine-pointed star, the points of which reach to the circumference of the medal. The triangular spaces between the points of the star contain the nine letters of the word "ABYSSINIA." On the obverse there is a laurel wreath, inside of which are the name, rank, and ship or regiment of the recipient in raised letters. The medal is surmounted by an Imperial crown, and a large silver ring through which the ribbon passes. It was awarded to the soldiers and sailors who took part in the Abyssinian operations of 1867–68, which resulted in the capture of Magdala. It is the only medal on which the name of the recipient is embossed on the reverse, the usual custom being for the name, rank, etc., of the recipient to be engraved upon the rim.

65.

66. ASHANTEE MEDAL. 1873–74.—This medal was given to all the men of Her Majesty's Forces who were employed on the Gold Coast during the operations against the King of Ashantee, 1873–74. The obverse bears the head of Queen Victoria with the usual wording, and the reverse a scene in high relief, representing a fight in the bush between British soldiers and a party of natives. The design, which is considered by experts to be one of the finest seen on British medals, was executed by Sir Edwin Poynter, R.A. A plain silver clasp is provided for suspension from the ribbon. An engagement bar, inscribed "COOMASSIE," was awarded to all those who were present at the battle of Amoaful, and the actions between that place and Coomassie, including the capture of the latter. Also to those who, during the five days of those battles, were engaged north of the Prah in maintaining and protecting the lines of communication of the main army.

66.

66. EAST AND WEST AFRICA MEDAL. 1887–1900.—The Ashantee medal, 1873–74, was again made use of for many expeditions in East and West Africa between 1887 and 1900. It is impossible here to mention all these small campaigns, but the medal with the following bars was issued to the officers and men of the Navy and Army: "1887–8." For operations against the Yonnie tribe. Nov. 1887 to Jan. 1888. "WITU 1890." For Witu expedition of 1890, carried out by men from H.M. ships with marines. "1891–2." Expedition up the Gambia. "1892." Expeditions against Tambi, March–April;

against Toniataba, March–April, and against the Jebus, May. " WITU AUGUST 1893." For the Pumwani and Iongeni expeditions, carried out by 236 officers and men of H.M. ships *Blanche, Sparrow,* and *Swallow.* " JUBA RIVER 1893." For the expedition of Aug. 1893, carried out by 1 officer and 40 men of H.M. ships *Blanche.* " LIWONDI 1893." Feb.– March, 1893. 3 officers and 34 men of H.M. ships *Herald* and *Mosquito.* " LAKE NYASSA 1893." Nov. 1893. H.M. ships *Adventurer* and *Pioneer,* and 100 Sikhs. " 1893–4." 50 men of West India Regiment who took part in Gambia expedition, 1894. " GAMBIA 1894." Feb.– March. Men of H.M. ships *Alecto, Magpie, Raleigh, Satellite,* and *Widgeon.* " BENIN RIVER 1894." Aug.–Sept. 1894. H.M. ships *Alecto, Philomel, Phoebe,* and *Widgeon.* " BRASS RIVER 1895." Feb. 1895. H.M. ships *Barossa, St. George, Thrush,* and *Widgeon.* " 1896–97." " 1896–98." Operations in the Gold Coast, Lagos, Borgu, and in various other operations between 1896 and 1898. Recipient received a bar according to the date of the operations in which he had taken part. " 1896–99." To all officers and men on military duty in the northern territory of the Gold Coast, or in the Hinterland of Lagos, Nov. 1896–May, 1899. " NIGER 1897." Egbon, Bida and Ilorin expeditions. Jan.–Feb. 1897. " BENIN 1897." Benin expedition. Officers and men of H.M. ships *Forte, Philomel, St. George, Barrosa, Phoebe, Theseus, Widgeon, Magpie,* and *Alecto.* " DAWKITA 1897." To the men of the Gold Coast Constabulary engaged in the Defence of Dawkita. " 1897–98." Same as " 1896–98." " 1898." Same as " 1896–98." " SIERRA LEONE 1898–99." Military operations in Sierra Leone. Feb. 1898– March, 1899. " 1899." For Bula and other expeditions of 1899. " 1900." Munshi and Kaduna Expeditions, Jan.–May, 1900. Men already in possession of the medal received the bar only on taking part in a subsequent expedition. For one expedition, that against M'wele in 1895–96, the medal was issued with no bar, but with the word " M'wele " and the date impressed on the rim. This medal, with its familiar black and yellow ribbon, is  still worn by many officers and men of the Royal Navy, for the sailors in the men-of-war in East and West Africa were constantly employed in expeditions into the interior against rebellious chiefs. The pos- session of the medal usually means that the wearer has seen a good deal of hard bush fighting, for, as a rule, the decoration was not issued to those who had not served ashore, and had not been in action. As many as five bars are sometimes seen attached to the ribbon, while two, three, and four are by no means rare.

67. MEDAL FOR AFGHANISTAN. 1878–80. —The obverse has the usual head of Queen Victoria, with the legend " Victoria Regina et Imperatrix." On the reverse a column of British troops are shown on the march. They are accompanied by native cavalry, and an officer rides in the foreground. In the centre is an elephant carrying a mountain-gun on his back. A mountain with a castle on its summit is in the background. The word " Afghanistan " appears round the top

67.

circumference, and below the dates " 1878–9–80." The medal hangs from its ribbon by a plain silver clasp. The following engagement bars were issued : " ALI-MUSJID." For the capture of Ali Musjid, Nov. 21st, 1878. " PEIWAR-KOTAL." For the forcing of the Peiwar Kotal of Dec. 2nd, 1878. " CHARASIA." For the action of Oct. 6th, 1879. " AHMED-KHEL." For battle of April 19th, 1880. " KABUL." For the operations at and around Kabul, Dec. 10th to 23rd, 1879. " KANDAHAR." To the troops under Sir Frederick Roberts' command who fought in the action against Sirdar Mahomed Ayub Khan on Sept. 1st, 1880. It was first proposed to issue the " India Medal, 1854," with bars for " Afghanistan," " Ali Musjid," and " Peiwar Kotal," for this campaign, but Queen Victoria subsequently decided to give a separate medal. The crimson in the ribbon is said to represent the heraldic colour of Great Britain, and the green the sacred colour of the Prophet.

52. KABUL TO KANDAHAR STAR. 1880. This decoration consists of a bronze, five-pointed star with radiations. In the inner angles of the points a small ball. In the centre of the star the Imperial cypher " V.R.I. " encircled by the words " KABUL TO KANDAHAR." The back of the star is plain bronze with a hollow centre, and is generally inscribed with the name, rank, and regiment of the recipient. The star is surmounted by a crown and a ring, and the ribbon for suspension passes through the latter. No bars were issued. The decoration was given to all the troops who took part in Lord Roberts' celebrated march from Kabul to Kandahar, August 3rd to 31st, 1880, and the bronze of which it is made came from guns taken from Ayoob Khan at the battle of Kandahar, September 1st, 1880.

52.

68. CAPE OF GOOD HOPE GENERAL SERVICE MEDAL.—On the obverse is the head of Queen Victoria with the legend, " Victoria Regina et Imperatrix." On the reverse are the arms of Cape Colony, with the words " Cape of Good Hope " round the top circumference. The medal hangs from its ribbon by means of a straight clasp, and was issued by the Cape of Good Hope Government in 1900, with the approval of the home Government. It was awarded to the Colonial troops and to a small number of British officers and men who took part in the Basutoland and Transkei operations of 1880–1, and in Bechuanaland in 1896–7. Three bars were awarded: " BASUTOLAND," " TRANSKEI," and " BECHUANALAND."

68.

69. EGYPTIAN MEDAL. 1882–1889.—The obverse bears the head of Queen Victoria with the usual legend, " Victoria Regina et

Imperatrix," and the reverse a representation of the Sphinx on a pedestal, with the word " Egypt" above it. The medal issued in 1882 bears the date on the reverse, but in subsequent issues the date is omitted. It hangs from its ribbon by a straight clasp. The medal was awarded to all soldiers and sailors who took part in the operations in Egypt and the Soudan, 1882–1889, and the blue and white stripes in the ribbon are sometimes said to typify the Blue and White Niles. The following bars were issued: " ALEXANDRIA, 11th July." To those present at the bombardment of Alexandria. " TEL-EL-KEBIR." For the engagement of September 13th, 1882. " SUAKIN, 1884."

69.

To those who were landed at Suakin or Trinkitat between February 19th and March 26th, 1884, and had already received the 1882 medal. Those who had not been awarded the '82 medal received a medal with no bar. " EL-TEB." To those present at the battle on February 29th, 1884. " TAMAAI." To those present at the battle of March 13th, 1884. " EL-TEB. TAMAAI." To those present at both the above battles. " THE NILE. 1884–85." To those officers and men who served south of Assouan on or before March 7th, 1885. " ABU KLEA." To those who fought in the battle of January 17th, 1885. " KIRBEKAN." For the battle of February 10th, 1885. " SUAKIN, 1885." To those who were engaged in the operations at Suakin between March 1st and May 14th, 1885. " TOFREK." For the action of March 22nd, 1885. " GEMAIZAH, 1888." To those who were landed at Suakin before the battle of Gemaizah on December 20th, 1888, and were present at the engagement. " TOSKI 1889." For the battle of Toski, August 3rd, 1889. Many medals without bars were issued to the soldiers serving in Egypt, and to the sailors who served on board ships in Egyptian waters.

70. NORTH-WEST CANADA. 1885.— The obverse of this medal bears the head of Queen Victoria with the words, " Victoria Regina et Imperatrix." The reverse has the words, " North-West Canada, 1885," surrounded by a wreath of maple. The medal hangs from its ribbon by a plain silver bar. The decoration was given by the home Government to the Canadian troops who were engaged in suppressing Riel's rebellion in North-West Canada in 1885. No British troops took part in the expedition. One bar, " SASKATCHEWAN," was awarded to those men who were present at the battle of that name.

70.

71. MEDALS AWARDED BY CHARTERED COMPANY OF SOUTH AFRICA FOR SERVICE IN MATABELELAND, 1893; RHODESIA, 1896; and MASHONALAND, 1897.—The obverse bears the head of Queen Victoria with the usual legend, and the reverse

shows the British lion charging and trampling upon native weapons.
The lion is wounded in front by an assegai. In the background a

bush. Above "Matabeleland, 1893," "Rhodesia,
1896," or "Mashonaland, 1897," as the case may
be. Below "British South Africa Company."
The medal hangs from an ornamental floreated
clasp. The Matabeleland medal was given to those
Imperial and Colonial troops who were engaged
with the Matabele under King Lobengula between
October and December, 1893. That for Rhodesia
was awarded to those who served in the operations
in that place between March and December, 1896,
and that for Mashonaland to those who took part
in the expeditions and operations of 1897. Men
who were already in possession of the medal

received bars inscribed, "RHODESIA, 1896," or
"MASHONALAND, 1897," for the subsequent operations. The cost of the medal was defrayed by the
Chartered Company of South Africa, but its issue
was sanctioned by Queen Victoria.

71.

72. ASHANTI STAR. 1896.—This decoration
was awarded to the officers and men who took
part in the expedition of 1895–96 to suppress slavery
and human sacrifices, and to punish King Prempeh
for his refusal to carry out his part of the treaty of 1874. The force had
a very difficult march through swamps and dense forests, but the King
was compelled to render public submission to the Governor, and,

with his principal chiefs, was made a prisoner
and deported. The bad climate occasioned many
deaths, and Prince Henry of Battenberg was one
of the victims. It is understood that Princess
Henry designed the bronze star which was awarded
by the Queen for the expedition. It consists of
a four-pointed star with a St. Andrew's cross
between the arms. In the centre of the obverse
is a crown encircled by a band, on which are
the word "Ashanti" and the date "1896."
The reverse is plain, but bears the words "From
the Queen." The star is surmounted by a ring
through which the ribbon passes, and no engagement bars were
issued.

72.

73. INDIA MEDAL. 1895.—The obverse bears the effigy of
Queen Victoria with the legend "Victoria Regina et Imperatrix." The
reverse shows a British and an Indian soldier each supporting the
British standard. At the sides the word "India" and the date
"1895." An ornamental scroll clasp is provided for suspension. This
medal—sanctioned in 1896—owed its origin to the Chitral Expedition
of 1895. The India General Service medal of 1854 had been issued
with no less than twenty-three different bars between the date of its
institution and 1895, and as many officers and men were in possession

of it with as many as five or ten of its different bars, it had lost, in their eyes, a considerable amount of its value as a record of their campaigns. It was considered, therefore, that the time had come to start a new one. For the Chitral campaign, accordingly, the new medal was issued with bars for " DEFENCE OF CHITRAL 1895 " and " RELIEF OF CHITRAL 1895." In 1898 it was again given with bars " PUNJAB FRONTIER 1897-8," " MALAKAND 1897," " SAMANA 1897," and " TIRAH 1897-8," to the officers and men who had taken part in the different expeditions. Again, in March, 1903, with King Edward's effigy on the obverse and a bar inscribed " WAZIRISTAN 1901-2," it was awarded for the operations carried out between November, 1901, and the following February. Those officers and men who had already received Queen Victoria's medal were awarded the bar only.

73.

74. CENTRAL AFRICA MEDAL. 1891–1898.—The obverse and reverse are exactly the same as those of the Ashantee medal, 1874, but as the ribbon is different it is held to be a separate decoration. The first medal, sanctioned in 1895, was awarded for various expeditions in Eastern and Central Africa between 1891 and 1894. No bars were given, and there was a ring in the top of the medal through which the ribbon passed. The greatest number of recipients were members of native regiments and their British officers, so the medal is rather rare. In 1899 the same medal was again issued for operations in British Central Africa between 1894 and 1898. This time, however, it was fitted with a plain silver clasp for suspension, while a bar inscribed " CENTRAL AFRICA 1894–1898 " was added.

Those officers and men who had already received the 1891–94 medal received the bar only, and had the rings of their medals removed and the plain silver clasp for suspension substituted. The black in this ribbon is said to allude to the Zanzibar troops employed in the expeditions ; the terra-cotta, to the Sikhs ; and the white, to the Europeans.

75. SOUDAN MEDAL. 1896–97.—This medal has a half-length figure of Queen Victoria on the obverse with the words " Victoria Regina et Imperatrix." On the reverse appears a seated figure of Victory and a trophy of draped flags. The figure holds in her right hand a palm leaf, and in her left a wreath of olives. Below is the word " Sudan." The medal hangs from a plain clasp, and no engagement bars were awarded. The black in this ribbon is said to represent the dervish enemy ; the yellow, the desert ; and the scarlet stripe, the " thin red line " of British troops. The medal was given in

75.

1899 and was bestowed on all those who had taken part in the operations for the reconquest of the Soudan.

76. EAST AND CENTRAL AFRICA MEDAL. 1899.—The obverse of this medal is exactly the same as that of the Soudan medal

for 1896–97 just described. The reverse has a standing figure of Britannia with a trident in her right hand and a palm branch and scroll in her left. The left arm is extended towards the sun which is just rising over the horizon. The British lion stands beside the figure of Britannia, and the words "East and Central Africa" appear below. The medal hangs from a straight clasp. It was given to the soldiers employed in the military operations in Uganda in 1897–98; to those who took part in the expedition against the Ogaden Somalis, April to August, 1898; and to those troops employed in the operations against Kabarega in Uganda between March and May, 1899.

The following bars were issued: "LUBWA's." For those who took part in the expedition against the Soudanese mutineers. September, 1897, to February, 1898. "UGANDA 1897–8." To those who took part in military operations in Uganda between July, 1897, and March, 1898. "1898." For the

76.

expedition against the Ogaden Somalis, April–August, 1898. "UGANDA 1899." To those employed in the expeditions against Kabarega. This medal superseded the Central Africa Medal, 1891–98.

77. ROYAL NIGER COMPANY'S MEDAL. 1899.—Following the example of the British South Africa Company, the Royal Niger Company, in 1899, decided, with Government approval, to issue a medal to those troops and constabulary who had taken part in expeditions in their territory between 1886 and 1897. The medal was only given to men who had been in expeditions in which casualties had occurred, and was awarded in silver to Europeans, and in bronze to natives. For the silver medal, one bar, inscribed "NIGERIA 1886–1897" was issued. The medal itself bears on its obverse the head of Queen Victoria wearing a wreath of laurel, with the words "Victoria Regina et Imperatrix." On the reverse is a shield in-

scribed with the words "Pax," "Jus," and "Ars," the three words forming the letter Y. Behind the shield is a trophy of swords, guns, and flags, and

77.

the whole design is surrounded by a wreath of laurel. This medal is very rare indeed in the British Army. The bar issued for the bronze medal bears the word "NIGERIA" only.

78. SOUTH AFRICAN MEDAL. 1899–1902.—This medal bears on one side the head of Queen Victoria with the customary legend. On the reverse there is a figure of Britannia with a flag in her left hand, and extending her right hand with a laurel wreath towards an advancing party of soldiers. In the background is the sea with men-of-war upon it. Above are the words "South Africa." The medal hangs from a plain silver clasp. It was granted to all officers and men of the Navy and Army, and to all hospital nurses, who actually served in South Africa between October 11th, 1899, and May 31st, 1902. Also to troops in Cape Colony and Natal at the outbreak of hostilities, and to the soldiers guarding Boer prisoners at St. Helena between April 14th, 1900, and May 31st, 1902. A similar medal with the same ribbon, but with the word "Mediterranean" on the reverse, was given to the officers and men of the Militia battalions who served in the Mediterranean garrisons during the war. It is impossible to give full details of all the different actions for which bars were awarded, but the following were issued: "CAPE COLONY," "NATAL," "RHODESIA," "RELIEF OF MAFEKING," "DEFENCE OF KIMBERLEY," "TALANA," "ELANDSLAAGTE," "DEFENCE OF LADYSMITH," "BELMONT," "MODDER RIVER," "TUGELA HEIGHTS," "RELIEF OF KIMBERLEY," "PAARDEBERG," "ORANGE FREE STATE," "RELIEF OF LADYSMITH," "DRIEFONTEIN," "WEPENER," "DEFENCE OF MAFEKING," "TRANSVAAL," "JOHANNESBURG," "LAING'S NEK," "DIAMOND HILL," "WITTEBERGEN," "BELFAST," "SOUTH AFRICA 1901," "SOUTH AFRICA 1902." The bars "South Africa 1901" and "South Africa 1902" were awarded to those officers and men who had served in South Africa during those years, but who were not eligible for the medal subsequently given by King Edward (see the next medal described). The "Cape Colony," "Natal," "Orange Free State," and "Transvaal" bars were given to troops who were employed in the places named between certain dates who did not receive any other bar for an engagement in Cape Colony, Natal, the Orange Free State, or the Transvaal. Nobody, however, could be awarded both the "Natal" and "Cape Colony" bars. All the officers and men in the ships on the Cape of Good Hope station received the medal, but those who did not land on duty received it without bars. The ribbon of this medal, red, blue, and orange, is frequently seen on the breasts of old soldiers who have rejoined the Army for the present war.

78.

79. KING EDWARD'S SOUTH AFRICAN MEDAL. 1901-1902. —The obverse of this medal has the head of King Edward VII. with the legend "Edwardus VII. Rex. Imperator." The reverse and mounting are the same as Queen Victoria's medal for the same campaign. It was given to all officers and men, doctors, and nursing sisters who were actually serving in South Africa on or after January 1st, 1902, provided they had completed eighteen months' war service on that date, or afterwards completed it before June 1st, 1902. Bars inscribed "SOUTH AFRICA 1901" and "SOUTH AFRICA 1902" were given with it, and those who did not qualify for the King's medal were eligible to receive them with their Queen's medals. The green, white, and orange ribbon of King Edward's South African medal is never seen except in conjunction with the red, blue, and orange ribbon of the Queen's, for if a man was awarded the former, he must also have been eligible for the latter. Very few King's medals are seen in the Royal Navy, for by the middle of 1901 most of the naval brigades had returned to their ships, and men who were not ashore on war service did not receive them.

80. CHINA MEDAL. 1900.—This medal was sanctioned in 1902 for the men of the Navy and Army who had been employed in North China during the so-called " Boxer Rebellion " of 1900. It was given to all officers and men who were employed in North China and in the valley of the Yang-tse-Kiang between June 11th and December 31st, 1900, and also to those Indian troops who served in China under the orders of General Sir A. Gaselee. The medal bears on the obverse the head of Queen Victoria with the usual legend, while the reverse is the same as for the China medal of 1842, with the date altered to " 1900." It is suspended from its ribbon by means of a plain silver clasp. The following bars were issued : " TAKU FORTS." To those engaged in the capture of the forts at the mouth of the Peiho, June 17th, 1900. " DEFENCE OF LEGATIONS." To those who defended the Pekin Legations between June 10th and August 14th, 1900. " RELIEF OF PEKIN." To those employed ashore in the operations between June 10th and August 14th, 1900, which culminated in the relief of Pekin. Many men in the Navy possess the China medal, but the greater number of them have no bars, which means that the recipients did not actually land on active service.

81. ASHANTI MEDAL. 1901.—This medal was sanctioned in October, 1901, and was granted to the men of the Ashanti Field Force who were employed in quelling the rebellion of the native tribes between March 31st and December 25th, 1900. During this time, also, the capital, Kumassi, was besieged by the rebels. The medal has on its obverse the bust of King Edward with the usual wording, and on the reverse a representation of the British lion looking to the left towards a rising sun. A native shield and two spears lie at the feet of the lion, and below, in an oblong, is the word " Ashanti." A plain silver clasp is provided for suspension from the ribbon. A bar, inscribed " KUMASSI," was given to those who took part in the defence and relief of that place.

81.

82.

82. AFRICA GENERAL SERVICE MEDAL. 1902.—The obverse of this medal is the same as that of the Ashanti medal just described, while the reverse is identical with that of the East and Central Africa of 1899, but with the word " Africa." It is suspended from its ribbon by means of a plain silver clasp. The medal, as its name implies, was awarded for all the expeditions and small wars in

Africa carried out by the Navy and Army between 1901 and the time of King Edward's death. It is impossible to give the details of all these different expeditions, but the following bars were awarded: " N. NIGERIA," for operations of 1900–1; " N. NIGERIA 1902 "; " N. NIGERIA 1903 "; " N. NIGERIA 1903–4 "; " N. NIGERIA 1904 "; " N. NIGERIA 1906 "; " S. NIGERIA," for operations of 1901 ; " S. NIGERIA 1902 "; " S. NIGERIA 1902–3 "; " S. NIGERIA 1903 "; " S. NIGERIA 1903–4 "; " S. NIGERIA 1904 "; " S. NIGERIA 1904–5 "; " S NIGERIA 1905 "; " S. NIGERIA 1905–6 "; " EAST AFRICA 1902 "; " EAST AFRICA 1904 "; " EAST AFRICA 1905 "; " EAST AFRICA 1906 "; " WEST AFRICA 1906 "; " WEST AFRICA 1908 "; " SOMALILAND 1901 "; " SOMALILAND 1902–4 "; " SOMALILAND 1908–10 "; " JUBALAND "; " UGANDA 1900 "; " B.C.A. 1899–1900 "; " GAMBIA "; " ARO 1901–1902 "; " LANGO 1901 "; " JIDBALLI "; " KISSI 1905 "; " NANDI 1905–6." This medal, with various of the bars, is frequently seen worn by naval officers and men. It is rarer in the Army, but has been bestowed upon many of the West African troops and men of different Indian regiments.

Another issue of the Africa General Service Medal with the effigy and titular legend of King George V. on the obverse was sanctioned in 1916. The medal is not issued without bars, and the following bars were authorised. " SHIMBER BERRIS 1914–15," to all officers and men who took part in the operations against the dervishes at Shimber Berris, Somaliland, 19th–25th Nov., 1914, and 2nd–9th Feb., 1915. " NYASALAND 1915," to the forces engaged in the operations against the rebels in the Shire Highlands of Nyasaland between 24th Jan. and 17th Feb., 1915. Recipients already in possession of King Edward's medal received the new bars only. A new bar, " EAST AFRICA 1913–14," was sanctioned in 1916.

N.B.—The Africa General Service Medal is never seen without a bar.

83. MEDAL FOR ZULU RISING IN NATAL. 1906.—A silver medal was granted by the Natal Government in 1908 to all those who had taken part in suppressing the native revolt of 1906. It hangs from a straight clasp, and has on the obverse a bust of King Edward with the usual wording, and on the reverse an erect female figure representing Natal with the sword of justice in her right hand and a palm branch in the left. She treads upon a heap of native weapons, and is supported by Britannia, who holds the Orb of Empire in her left hand. In the background there is a group of natives, while the sun is bursting forth from behind receding storm clouds. One bar, inscribed " 1906," was issued with the medal.

83.

84. TIBET MEDAL. 1903–4.—This medal was awarded to all members of the Tibet Mission and the accompanying troops who served at, or beyond, Siliguri, between December 13th, 1903, and September 23rd, 1904. The medal bears on the obverse the head of King

Edward VII., with the usual inscription, and on the reverse the representation of a fort on a hill with "Tibet 1903-4" below. A silver

scroll clasp is provided for suspension. A bar inscribed "GYANTSE" was given with the medal to all those who were present at the operations near Gyantse between May 3rd and July 6th, 1904. Comparatively few British troops received this medal, so that it is rarely seen in Great Britain.

84.

85. INDIA GENERAL SERVICE MEDAL. 1908.—In December 1908, a new Indian General Service Medal was issued for the North-West Frontier campaign of that year. It bears the bust of King Edward in military uniform, with the legend "Edwardus VII. Kaisar-i-Hind." The reverse shows a fort on a hill-top with mountains in the background, and below the word "India" inside

branches of oak and laurel. The medal hangs from an ornamental scroll clasp, and one bar, "NORTH WEST FRONTIER 1908," was granted. It was the last medal issued during the reign of King Edward. After the Abor Expedition of 1911–12, the same medal, but with King George's effigy on the obverse, was issued to the troops who had taken part. A bar inscribed "ABOR 1911–12" was awarded with it, and those men who already possessed King Edward's medal received the bar only.

85.

86. NAVAL GENERAL SERVICE MEDAL. 1915.—This medal was established by King George in 1915, "to be awarded for service in minor naval operations, whether in the nature of belligerency or police, which may be considered of sufficient importance to justify the award of a medal in cases where no other medal would be appropriate. The medal will have a distinctive ribbon, white with crimson borders, and two crimson stripes, and a clasp with appropriate wording." At the time of its establishment the clasp inscribed "PERSIAN GULF, 1909–1914," was authorised to be issued with the medal to the officers and men of H.M. ships who were employed in the operations for the suppression of the arms traffic in the Arabian Sea or Persian Gulf, north of Latitude 22°, north and west of Longitude 64° east, between October 19th, 1909, and August 1st, 1914. The obverse bears the head of King George in naval uniform with the usual legend, and the reverse

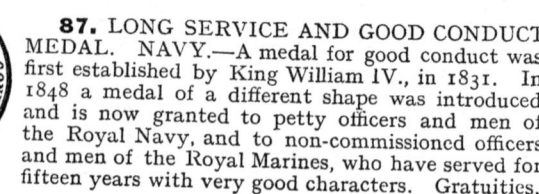

a representation of Britannia and two sea-horses travelling through the sea.

87. LONG SERVICE AND GOOD CONDUCT MEDAL. NAVY.—A medal for good conduct was first established by King William IV., in 1831. In 1848 a medal of a different shape was introduced and is now granted to petty officers and men of the Royal Navy, and to non-commissioned officers and men of the Royal Marines, who have served for fifteen years with very good characters. Gratuities,

87.

varying with the rank of the recipients, may also be granted. The medal, which hangs from a straight clasp, bears on its obverse the bust of the King in naval uniform, and on the reverse the representation of an old-fashioned line-of-battle ship at anchor. The ship is surrounded by a rope cable tied in a reef knot at the bottom, and round the circumference outside the rope are the words " For Long Service and Good Conduct."

88. LONG SERVICE AND GOOD CONDUCT MEDAL. ARMY. —This medal was also instituted by King William IV. in 1830. It is now awarded to non-commissioned officers and men of the British Army after eighteen years' service with irreproachable character with a gratuity of £5. Warrant Officers also receive the medal, but without gratuity. The medal hangs from an ornamental scroll clasp, and has on one side the effigy of the reigning Sovereign in Field Marshal's uniform, and on the other the inscription, " For Long Service and Good Conduct." *

88.

88, 89. MERITORIOUS SERVICE MEDAL. ARMY AND ROYAL MARINES.—This medal was instituted in 1845 for the Army, and four years later for the Royal Marines. It is awarded to Sergeants of the Army and Royal Marines as rewards for meritorious or distinguished service, in peace or in war. It is only given on very rare occasions, and may not be worn with the Long Service and Good Conduct Medal. A sum of £4000 a year is at the disposal of the War Office, and £400 a year at the disposal of the Admiralty, to be granted in annuities with the medal, but the annuities are not allowed to exceed £20 a year each. In the case of the Royal Marines the medals are only granted to Sergeants who have completed twenty-one years' service, or have been granted a life pension on account of wounds received in action or on duty, and as only a certain number of them can be awarded, they are very rarely seen. The regulations for the Army are very similar. The decoration has on the obverse the effigy of the reigning Sovereign, and on the reverse the words " For Meritorious Service," surrounded by two branches of laurel, and surmounted by the Imperial crown. It is worn on the left breast; is hung from an ornamental clasp: and the ribbon is crimson * for the Army, and dark blue for the Royal Marines (No. **89**).

90. DECORATION FOR OFFICERS OF THE ROYAL NAVAL RESERVE.—This Decoration may be conferred upon Commissioned Officers of the Royal Naval Reserve after fifteen years' service as such. The design is very similar to that of the Volunteer Officers' Decoration of 1892. The letters " R.D." are inserted in the Navy List against the

---

* In June, 1916, the ribbon for the Army Long Service and Good Conduct and Meritorious Service Medals was altered from plain crimson to crimson with white edges. The new ribbon was taken into wear by all officers, warrant officers, N.C.Os., and men in possession of the medals who were then serving. The old type of the ribbon is shown as No. 26a, p. 11.

names of officers who have received the Decoration. The ribbon is the same as that of the R.N.R. Long Service and Good Conduct medal, but is one and a half inches wide instead of one and a quarter inches.

90. DECORATION FOR OFFICERS OF THE ROYAL NAVAL VOLUNTEER RESERVE.—Commissioned Officers of the R.N. Volun-

teer Reserve, similarly, may be granted a decoration, designated " The Volunteer Officer's Decoration," after twenty years' service. The letters " V.D." are inserted in the Navy List against the names of officers who have received it.

90. ROYAL NAVAL RESERVE LONG SER-VICE AND GOOD CONDUCT MEDAL.—This medal may be granted to men of the Royal Naval Reserve who satisfactorily complete fifteen years' service, with the necessary periods of naval training, provided their characters have never been assessed below " V.G." The medal bears on one side the bust of His Majesty in naval uniform, and on the other a representation of a battleship, with the legend " Diuturne fidelis." It hangs from its green ribbon by a straight clasp.

90.

90. ROYAL NAVAL VOLUNTEER RESERVE LONG SERVICE MEDAL.—Members of the Royal Naval Volunteer Reserve may also be granted a medal for long service after twelve years. Previous service in the Volunteer or Territorial forces, including service in a Cadet Corps or Cadet Battalion, from the age of fifteen is also allowed to count. The medal is similar to that for the Royal Naval Reserve.

90. VOLUNTEER OFFICERS' DECORATION. 1892.—This decoration was instituted in July, 1892, for the purpose of rewarding

" efficient and capable " officers of the Volunteer Force who had served for twenty years. Two years later a similar distinction was introduced for officers of volunteer forces in India and the Colonies, but in the case of India the qualifying service was reduced to eighteen years. The badge consists of an oval oak wreath in silver, tied in gold, and having in the centre the Royal cypher surmounted by the Imperial Crown, both in gold. It is suspended from its ribbon by a silver ring, while the ribbon itself is one and a half inches wide, and has a silver bar brooch with oak leaves at the top. In the decoration for British volunteer officers the cypher was

90.

" V.R." or " E.R. VII." according to the reign in which it was issued, while that for Indian and Colonial officers had " V.R.I." of " E.R.I. VII." The award of the decoration entitled the recipient to use the letters " V.D." after his name. The V.D., except for India, became obsolete when the volunteer force was disbanded in 1908.

90. COLONIAL OFFICERS' AUXILIARY FORCES DECORA-TION.—This decoration was established in 1899 for commissioned officers in the Colonial Auxiliary Forces who had served for twenty

years, service on the West Coast of Africa counting double. It
superseded the V.D. for colonial officers. The oval badge has in
the centre the Imperial cypher "E.R.I. VII.," or
"G.R.I. V.," as the case may be. The cypher is
surrounded by a band bearing the words "Colonial
Auxiliary Forces," while the badge is surmounted by
an Imperial Crown. It hangs from a green ribbon
one and a quarter inches wide, by means of a straight
silver clasp.

90.

90. VOLUNTEER LONG SERVICE MEDAL.
1894.—This medal was instituted in 1894 for men of
the Volunteer Forces who had completed twenty
years' service. In 1896 its issue was extended to
the Indian and Colonial forces, eighteen years service
being the qualification in India. The medal, which
hangs from a straight clasp and a green ribbon one
and a quarter inches wide, has on the obverse the effigy
of the reigning Sovereign, with the usual legend. The obverse has laurel
branches and intertwined scrolls bearing the words,
"For Long Service in the Volunteer Force." In
the Indian and Colonial medals the obverse had
"et Imperatrix," or "et Imperator," added to the
legend. This medal became obsolete in Great
Britain on the disbandment of the volunteers in
1908, but, with the effigy of the reigning Sovereign
on the obverse, the words on the reverse altered
to "For Long Service in the Colonial Auxiliary
Forces," and the laurel branches surmounted by
the Imperial Crown, is still issued in the Colonies.
The Honourable Artillery Company have a special
ribbon for this medal. It is half dark blue, half scarlet, with narrow
yellow edges.

90.

91. TERRITORIAL DECORATION.—This decoration, instituted to replace the Volunteer Officers'
Decoration of 1892, when the Territorial Force was
established, is of much the same design as the V.D.
It has the cypher "E.R. VII.," or "G.R. V.," according to the reign in which it was issued, and hangs
from a green ribbon, one and a half inches wide, with
a yellow stripe down the centre. Recipients are
entitled to use the letters "T.D." after their names.
It is stated that the officers of the H.A.C. wear the
special ribbon mentioned above with this decoration.

91. TERRITORIAL EFFICIENCY MEDAL.—
This medal was instituted by King Edward on the
establishment of the Territorial Force in 1908-9. It
really superseded the old Volunteer Long Service
medal, and is awarded to men of the Territorial Force
after twelve years' service, provided they have under-
gone at least twelve trainings. The medal, which is

91.

oval, bears on its obverse the head of the reigning Sovereign with the usual legend. On the reverse it has the inscription "Territorial Force Efficiency Medal." The ribbon is the same as for the Territorial Officers' Decoration, but is one and a quarter inches in width instead of one and a half inches. The ribbon passes through a ring in the top of the medal. The H.A.C. wear their special ribbon with this medal, as it is the modern counterpart of the Volunteer L.S. Medal 1894.

92. IMPERIAL YEOMANRY LONG SERVICE AND GOOD CONDUCT MEDAL.—Formerly given to members of the Imperial Yeomanry after ten years' service with a minimum of ten trainings. It is oval, and bears on one side the head of the reigning Sovereign, and on the other, "Imperial Yeomanry. For Long Service and Good Conduct." It hangs by a ring from a yellow ribbon. It is now obsolete, those entitled to it receiving the Territorial Force Efficiency Medal.

93. MILITIA LONG SERVICE AND GOOD CONDUCT MEDAL. —This medal was granted by King Edward to all non-commissioned officers and men of good character in the Militia who were serving on, or after, November 9th, 1904. Eighteen years' service and at least

93.

fifteen annual trainings were required to qualify for it. It is oval, and has on its obverse the head of King Edward with the usual legend, and on the reverse the words "Militia. For Long Service and Good Conduct." It hangs from a light blue ribbon by a ring in the top of the medal.

94. SPECIAL RESERVE LONG SERVICE AND GOOD CONDUCT MEDAL.—Granted to members of the Special Reserve of the Army after a certain number of years service with good character. It is similar to the Territorial Efficiency Long Service and Good Conduct medal, but has different wording on the reverse, and hangs from a dark blue ribbon with a light blue stripe.

INDIAN AND COLONIAL LONG SERVICE AND GOOD CONDUCT MEDALS.

88. India. **95.** Cape of Good Hope. **96.** Tasmania. **97.** West African Frontier Force and King's African Rifles. **98.** Australian Commonwealth. **99.** New South Wales. **100.** Queensland. **101.** Natal. **102.** Permanent Overseas Forces. The ribbon for the Canadian Forces is the same as No. 95, except that the central stripe is white, while that for New Zealand Forces has a narrow central green stripe.

A medal for Long Service and Good Conduct is awarded to native troops in India in much the same conditions as in the Imperial Forces. It hangs from the same ribbon, and has the same clasp, as the medal for the British Army. The obverse, however, has the inscription "Kaisar-I-Hind," as well as the effigy of the reigning Sovereign, while on the reverse there is a wreath of lotus flowers and leaves encircling one of palm leaves. Between the wreaths is the circular inscription, " For Long Service and Good Conduct," and inside the inner palm wreath is the word " India." Medals for Long Service and Good Conduct are also given to the men of permanently embodied Colonial troops. The medals are the same as for the British Army, except that the name of the Dominion, State, or Colony appears on the reverse above the inscription, " For Long Service and Good Conduct." The ribbons are crimson, but each Dominion or Colony has a stripe of a distinctive colour down the centre.

COLONIAL DISTINGUISHED CONDUCT MEDALS.—Medals for " Distinguished Conduct in the Field," for acts of gallantry in war, are also awarded to men of permanently embodied Colonial Forces. The medals are the same as those for the British soldiers, but the name of the Dominion or Colony appears on the reverse of the medal, while the ribbon is of a distinctive colour. Ribbon No. **103** shows the D.C.M. for the native troops of the West African Frontier Force and the King's African Rifles. The D.C.Ms. awarded to Colonial troops during the present war have been of the usual British pattern.

INDIAN AND COLONIAL MERITORIOUS SERVICE MEDALS. —Medals for Meritorious Service are awarded to native troops of the Indian Army, and to the men of permanently embodied Colonial Forces, in much the same way as in the British Army. That for the Indian Army is the same as the Indian Long Service and Good Conduct medal with the inscription on the reverse altered to " For Meritorious Service," and hangs from the usual crimson ribbon. The Colonial Meritorious Service medals, too, are the same as those for the British Army, except that the name of the Dominion, State, or Colony appears on the reverse above the crown. The ribbons are crimson with stripes of the distinctive colours as mentioned above. Ribbon No. **104** shows that of the Australian Commonwealth Meritorious Service medal.

105. TURKISH MEDAL FOR THE CRIMEAN WAR.—After the Crimean War, the Turkish Government presented a silver medal to certain of the soldiers and sailors of the Allied Forces—British, French, and Sardinians—who had taken part in the campaign. The medal bears on the obverse a field gun, upon which is spread a map of the Crimea. In the background are the British, French, Sardinian, and Turkish flags, and below is the inscription, " Crimea 1855 " in English, French, or Italian. The reverse has the Sultan's cypher within a laurel wreath, with the word " Crimea " in Turkish, and the date " 1271 " in Arabic. Permission to wear the medals was granted to the British recipients, and they were generally fitted with a ring for suspension, or else with silver clasps. The medals intended for the British had the British and Turkish flags to the fore on the obverse, with the inscription in English ; those for the French troops had the French and Turkish flags to the front, with the wording in French ; and those for the Sardinians the Sardinian and Turkish flags to the fore, and the inscription in Italian. Owing, however, to the ship bringing home the British medals being wrecked, many of our soldiers and sailors received French or Sardinian medals instead of the ones originally intended for them.

106. SARDINIAN MEDAL FOR CRIMEAN WAR.—After the Crimean War the King of Sardinia also awarded a silver medal to 450 specially selected officers and men of the Navy and Army. The obverse has the arms of Savoy, surmounted by the crown of Sardinia, within two branches of palm and olive. Round the circumference is the legend " Al Valore Militare." On the reverse is the name, and regiment or ship, of the recipient, within a laurel wreath, and outside the wreath are the words, " Spedizione d'oriente. 1855–56." The blue watered ribbon passes through a broad loop at the top of the medal.

107. MEDAL FOR CHITRAL CAMPAIGN GIVEN BY THE MAHARAJAH OF JUMMOO AND KASHMIR.—The Maharajah of Jummoo and Kashmir presented a bronze medal to certain British officers and to the men of the native levies (Irregular troops) who took part in the defence and relief of Chitral, 1895. The decoration is kidney shaped, and has on the obverse a coat of arms with two native soldiers as supporters, with, below, a native inscription on a scroll, and the words, " Jummoo and Kashmir." The reverse has a representation of a fortress with troops in the foreground. It hangs from its ribbon by an ornamental clasp exactly similar to that of the 1895 India medal, and has one bar inscribed, " CHITRAL 1895." This medal is not worn in uniform by British officers and men.

108. KHEDIVE'S BRONZE STAR. 1882–91.—The Khedive of Egypt presented a bronze star to every officer and man of the Navy and

108.

Army who had received the British war medal for the Egyptian campaigns, 1882–5. The decoration consists of a five-pointed bronze star, in the centre of which is a view of the Sphinx, with the desert and pyramids in the background. The view in the centre is surrounded by a circular band, on which are the words " Egypt 1882," above, and below, in Arabic, " Khedive of Egypt 1299." On the reverse is the Khedive's monogram surmounted by a crown. The star is suspended by a ring from an ornamental clasp, and in the centre of this clasp is a star and a crescent. The bronze star was first given for the 1882 campaign, but its issue was subsequently extended for the 1884, 1885, 1888–9,

and 1890 operations. The later stars are similar in appearance to the first, but bear the words " Egypt 1884," or " Egypt 1884–6," with the corresponding Arabic inscriptions. Stars bearing no dates were issued subsequent to 1886. Most of the troops engaged in the operations at Suakin in 1888–9, and on the Nile in 1889, had already received the decoration for the earlier campaigns, and as a second star was not issued to any one man, very few of the undated ones were issued. They are, therefore, rather rare. The bronze star, undated, but bearing a bronze bar with the inscription " TOKAR 1308 (*i.e.* A.H.)," in Arabic, was given in 1893 to British officers and Egyptian troops who fought in the battle of that name on Feb. 19th, 1891. The officers and men of H.M. ships *Dolphin* and *Sandfly*, who were on transport duty at the time, and the troops serving at Trinkitat on the day of the battle, received the star without bar. Queen Victoria's silver medal was not given in this case, and it is the only instance in which the star will be seen by itself.

109. KHEDIVE'S SUDAN MEDAL. 1896–1905.—In 1897 the Khedive of Egypt granted a silver medal to all British and Egyptian troops, and to officers and men of the Royal Navy, who had taken part in the Dongola campaign of 1896. The medal bears on one side an oval shield charged with stars and crescents, behind which is a trophy of weapons. On the reverse there is a Turkish inscription. It hangs from its ribbon by a straight silver clasp, and the yellow ribbon, with the broad blue watered stripe down the centre, is said to typify the desert with the Blue Nile flowing through it. The medal was again given for various other expeditions between 1896 and 1905, and the following bars were awarded between those dates, though medals with no bars were also given : " FIRKET." To those who took part in the operations south of Akasha on June 7th, 1896. " HAFIR." To those who took part in the operations south of Fareig on Sept. 19th, 1896. " The ATBARA." For the battle of April 8th, 1898. " KHARTOUM." For the battle of Sept. 2nd, 1898. " GEDAREF." For the capture of Gedaref and the subsequent engagements in the neighbourhood. " ABU-HAMED." For the battle of Aug. 7th, 1897. " SUDAN 1897." To those already in possession of the medal who were at, or south of, Kerma and No. 6 station between July 15th and Nov. 6th, 1897. " SUDAN 1899." For services in connection with the reconquest of the Dongola province. " GEDID." To all who took part in the actions there on Nov. 22nd and 24th, 1899. " BAHR-EL-GHAZEL 1900–2." For the operations resulting in the re-occupation of the province of that name. " JEROK." For the operations of 1904 in the Blue Nile Province. " NYAM-NYAM." For the expedition against the tribes of this name in the Bahr-el-Ghazal Province, 1905.

109.

110. SUDAN MEDAL. 1910.—This medal was awarded by the Khedive in 1911, was sanctioned by the British Government, and was presented to those troops who had taken part in the operations against the rebellious native tribes in the Atwot district of the Bahr-el-Ghazal province in February, March, and April, 1910. It was also given to those who took part in the operations against Jebel Tajoi in South Kordofan, November and December, 1910, and to officers and men who took part in various punitive expeditions in the Sudan in 1911 and 1912. The medal bears on one side the cypher of the Khedive, and the date ; and on the reverse is a lion standing in an

110

attitude of attention, with his fore paws resting upon a panel bearing the word " Sudan." Below is an oval native shield and spears. In the background is a representation of the River Nile, with the further bank and palm trees behind. Behind this again is the rising sun, spreading its rays across the sky. The medal hangs from a straight clasp, and bars inscribed " ATWOT," " S. KORDOFAN 1910," and " SUDAN 1912," in English and Arabic, were awarded with it to those who took part in the various expeditions.

111. MESSINA MEDAL.—This medal was awarded by the King of Italy to the officers and men of the British men-of-war, and to others, who assisted in succouring the injured after the terrible earthquake at Messina and Reggio in December, 1908. The medal, which is rather smaller than the majority of British specimens, bears on one side the effigy of the King of Italy, and on the other an inscription in Italian. A ring is provided for suspension. Officers and men of H.M. Navy and Army are permitted to wear this medal in uniform.

112. THE LEGION OF HONOUR.—The " Légion d'Honneur," was instituted by Napoleon Bonaparte, on May 19th, 1802, for rewarding distinguished military and civil services. Before this date there was no special reward which could be bestowed upon civilians, but swords of honour, muskets of honour, and other weapons could be granted to soldiers and sailors for gallantry in war. The original cross of the Legion of Honour was a white enamel gold badge, with five rays with double points, each point being tipped with a silver ball. Between the arms of the cross appeared a green enamel wreath of oak and laurel,

112.

while in the centre of the obverse, on a silver gilt ground, was the effigy of Napoleon, surrounded by a riband of blue enamel, with the inscription, " Napoleon. Empereur des Français," in gold lettering. The reverse was similar, but bore the Imperial eagle in the centre, with the words, " Honneur et Patrie," on the blue riband. The badge itself was surmounted by an Imperial crown for suspension. The present badge is much the same, but has on the obverse the female head symbolic of the Republic, surrounded by the blue riband bearing the words, " Republique Française. 1870." The reverse has two crossed tricoloured flags, with the wording " Honneur et Patrie." A green enamelled wreath is also provided for suspension in place of the crown. The Order is divided into five grades: " Grands Croix," " Grands Officiers," " Commandeurs," " Officiers," and " Chevaliers." A recipient must start in the lowest grade, *i.e.* as a " Chevalier," or Knight. Further, except in war, every grade must be passed through, and a " Chevalier " cannot become an " Officier " until he has done four years in the former grade; an Officier must wait for two years before he can be promoted to " Commandeur "; a " Commandeur " has to spend three years as such before he can be made a " Grand Officier "; and a " Grand Officier " must wait for five years before he is eligible for a

" Grand Croix." War service counts as double for these periods of qualification.

" GRAND CROIX " wear a gold badge suspended on the left hip by a broad scarlet watered ribbon passing over the right shoulder, and on the left breast a silver star.

" GRANDS OFFICIERS " wear the badge in gold hung round the neck, and on the right breast a silver star similar to that of the " Grand Croix."

" COMMANDEURS " wear the badge hung round the neck on a scarlet ribbon.

" OFFICIERS " wear the badge on the left breast suspended from a scarlet ribbon with a rosette in the centre.

" CHEVALIERS " wear a similar badge in the same place, but without the rosette on the ribbon.

The badge for "Chevaliers" is white enamel on silver, but all superior grades have it in white enamel on gold.

The Legion of Honour is the premier Order of the French Republic, and is only conferred for gallantry in action, or for twenty years' distinguished military or civil service in peace. The Order can be bestowed upon foreigners, notable cases of this having occurred during the present war when a Grand Croix was bestowed upon Field Marshal Sir John French, and the cross of a Chevalier upon the late Flight Sub-Lieut. Warneford, V.C., R.N.A.S., for destroying a German Zeppelin.

113. MEDAILLE MILITAIRE.—This medal is the French counterpart of our Distinguished Conduct Medal, and was established in 1852. It is only awarded to General Officers in command of armies—a recent case being its bestowal upon Field Marshal Sir John French, for services during the present war—and to non-commissioned officers and men of the Navy and Army who specially distinguish themselves in action. The decoration itself has a silver rim formed of a wreath of laurel leaves tied at top and bottom with narrow silver-gilt ribbons. In the centre of the obverse is a gilt female head symbolical of the Republic on a roughened gilt ground, the whole being surrounded by a narrow riband of blue enamel bearing the words " Republique Française. 1870 " in gilt letters. The centre of the reverse is inscribed with the words " Valeur et Discipline." Above the medal is a trophy of arms consisting of crossed cannons, a cuirass, anchor, swords, and muskets, and above this is the ring through which the orange, green-edged ribbon passes. The Medaille Militaire has been bestowed upon various British N.C.Os. and men during the present war.

113.

114. CROIX DE GUERRE.—This bronze cross was established by the French Government in a Law of April 8th, 1915, to commemorate individual mentions in despatches for the duration of the war. The cross is awarded to soldiers or

114.

sailors of all ranks, officers included, and also to officers and men of Allied forces, mentioned in French despatches, for an individual feat or arms mentioned in a despatch from the General Officer commanding an Army, Army Corps, Division, Brigade, or the C.O. of a Regiment, or the corresponding units of naval forces.

The different classes of despatches for which a recipient was awarded the Cross may be recognised by the following embellishments attached to the ribbon:—

Army Despatch . .	Small bronze laurel branch (Palme en bronze).
Army Corps Despatch .	Silver gilt star.
Divisional Despatch .	Silver star.
Brigade, Regimental, or similar unit Despatch	Bronze star.

Every time a man is mentioned he receives a corresponding sign. Thus a man may wear the Cross with, say, the silver star and the "Palme en bronze."

115.

115. ORDER OF ST. STANISLAS. (Russia.)—This order was founded in 1765, and consists of three classes: Knights Grand Cross, Commanders, and Companions. The badge is a gold, crimson enamelled Maltese cross, with double points, each point being tipped with a small gold ball. Between each arm of the cross is the white eagle of Poland in gold. In the centre, on a circular white enamel ground, are two branches of laurel, enamelled green, encircling two intertwined S's in gold. The Order of St. Stanislas was recently bestowed by the Czar upon certain officers of British regiments for their services during the present war.

116.

116. ORDER OF ST. GEORGE. (Russia.)—This Order was founded in 1769 by the Empress Catherine II., for rewarding military services exclusively, and it is now bestowed for bravery in action in much the same way as our Victoria Cross and D.S.O. The badge consists of a gold, white enamelled cross, pattée, with, in the centre, a representation of St. George fighting the dragon. There are four grades of the Order: Knights Grand Cross, Knights Commanders, Commanders, and Companions, while a similar silver cross, amounting to what is really the 5th class of the Order, and medals of the Order, are given to N.C.Os. and men of the Army and Navy for gallantry in action. The Order of St. George is occasionally bestowed upon foreigners, and it or the medals, were awarded by the Czar to Commander Max Horton, D.S.O., R.N., and to the crew of the British submarine, who torpedoed the German battleship *Pommern* in the Baltic, as well as to various officers and men of the British Expeditionary Force while serving in France.

117. ORDER OF LEOPOLD. (Belgium.)—This Order was instituted in 1832 by King Leopold I., and is sometimes conferred upon officers for gallantry in the field. The badge consists of a gold, white enamelled, Maltese cross with V-shaped extremities to its arms, resting upon a wreath of oak and laurel enamelled green. In the centre, on a circular black ground, is the rampant lion of Belgium in gold, surrounded by a circular crimson riband bearing the words " L'Union fait la force." The badge is surmounted by a gold crown, at the top of which is a ring through which the ribbon passes. The decorations awarded to military officers for services in the field have crossed swords between the cross and the crown, while those

117.

bestowed upon civilians in time of peace are without the swords. There are five classes of the Order.

118. ORDER OF THE RISING SUN. (Japan.)—This Order was founded in 1875, and comprises eight different classes, various of which are conferred upon officers, non-commissioned officers, or men of the Army or Navy for gallant service in war or for distinguished services in peace.

119. ORDER OF THE SACRED TREASURE. (Japan.)—This Order was instituted in 1888, and is frequently bestowed upon naval and military officers for long and meritorious service. It comprises five different classes, while a 6th class can be bestowed upon non-commissioned officers and men.

118.

119.

120. ORDER OF THE GOLDEN KITE. (Japan.)—The Order of the Golden Kite is the equivalent of our Victoria Cross, and as such is given for gallantry in action. There are various different classes, the higher grades being bestowed upon officers, and the lower upon non-commissioned officers and men.

121, 122. THE IRON CROSS. (Prussia.)—The Order of the Iron Cross was founded in 1813 to reward those who distinguished themselves in the war then in progress. It could be awarded either to the military or to civilians, irrespective of class. The only difference between the two decorations (*i.e.* Military and Civil) was in the colouring of the ribbon. After the close of the campaign mentioned above the award of the cross lapsed until 1870, when it was revived for the Franco-German War. The badge consists of a cast-iron cross pattée,

with a milled silver edge. That awarded in 1813 had a crown on the upper limb, three oak leaves and the date "1813" on the lower arm. That given for the 1870–71 war had the crown on the upper limb, the letter "W" in the centre, and the date "1870" on the lower limb. The Iron Crosses bestowed for the war now in progress are similar to those for the Franco-German campaign, but bear the date "1914." There are three classes of the Order :—

121.

THE GRAND CROSS, double the size of the ordinary cross, is worn round the neck, and is awarded solely for the winning of an important battle, the conquest of an important place, or the brave defence of a fortress.

THE FIRST AND SECOND CLASSES OF THE IRON CROSS are given for bravery in action, irrespective of rank. Knights of the 1st Class wear the cross suspended from the button-hole, and, in addition, a similar cross on the left breast. Knights of the 2nd Class of the Order wear the cross suspended from the button-hole.

Large numbers of Iron Crosses have been bestowed during the present war. The decoration is suspended from its ribbon by a silver ring, and the ribbon is black with white stripes towards either edge for military or naval recipients, and white with black stripes towards either edge for civilians.

ORDER OF MILITARY MERIT. (Prussia.) Ribbon similar to No. 121.—This Order was founded in 1665. The badge consists of a gold, eight-pointed cross, enamelled sky-blue, with a gold eagle between each of the arms. On the top arm of the cross is the letter "F" surmounted by a crown, and on the three other arms the words "Pour" —"le Mé-"—"rite." This Order is bestowed upon naval or military officers who render especially conspicuous service in war, and is worn round the neck from a broad black ribbon edged with white, similar

to No. 121. A civil class of the Order was instituted in 1842, but the badge consists of a circular medallion worked in gold and sky-blue enamel instead of the cross. It is rather strange to think that the inscription "Pour le Mérite" is in French.

123. THE ORDER OF THE MEDJIDIE. (Turkey.)—This Order was established in 1852, and has been bestowed upon British subjects in much the same way as the Osmanieh, though more frequently. Over a thousand British officers received the Order after the Crimean War. The badge is a cut-silver star of seven points, between the arms of which are seven small crescents and stars. In the centre is the Sultan's cypher on a gold or silver ground, and

123.

this is surrounded by a crimson riband with a Turkish inscription. A star and a crescent, enamelled crimson, are provided for suspension. There are five classes of the Order; the same as in the case of the Osmanieh.

124. THE ORDER OF THE OSMANIEH. (Turkey.)—The Order of the Osmanieh was founded in 1861 by the Sultan Abdul Aziz. It has been conferred upon many officers of the British Army for services in the various Sudan campaigns, and for their work in Egypt in times of peace, and upon several naval officers, notably certain of those who were lent to the Turkish Government some years ago for the reorganisation and training of the Turkish Fleet. The badge consists of a gold seven-pointed star enamelled green, with a gold ball on each point. Between each of the arms are three silver radiations. In the centre, on a ground of crimson enamel, is a Turkish inscription and a gold crescent, and this device is surrounded by a green enamel riband bearing another inscription in gold lettering. The reverse bears a trophy of Turkish flags and drums, and the date. The star hangs from its ribbon by means of a star and crescent and a ring. There are five classes of the Order, corresponding to

124.

Knights Grand Cross, Knights Commanders, Commanders, Officers and Companions.

125. MEDAILLE DE SAUVETAGE. (France.)—This medal, which has been awarded to certain British officers and men for gallantry in saving the lives of French subjects, corresponds to our Albert Medals, Royal Humane Society's Medals, Board of Trade Medal, and Foreign Office Medals for saving life at sea. There are five classes:

Gold Medal, 1st Class, with gold palm and button on the ribbon.

Gold Medal, 2nd Class, with silver palm and button on the ribbon.

125.

Silver Medal, 1st Class, with gold palm on the ribbon.

Silver Medal, 2nd Class, with silver palm on the ribbon.

Bronze Medal with bronze palm on the ribbon.

This medal is worn on the right breast by British subjects.

126. ORDER OF THE NILE. (Egypt.)—This Order was instituted by the present Sultan of Egypt in 1915 for rewarding those persons who have rendered useful service to the country. It is divided into five classes:—"Grands Cordons," "Grands Officiers," "Commandeurs," "Officiers," and "Chevaliers.'

Recipients of the GRAND CORDON wear a star on the left breast, and, on the left hip, the decoration hung from a broad ribbon of blue moirè, edged golden yellow, passing over the right shoulder.

F

GRAND OFFICIERS wear a smaller star on the right breast, with the decoration hung round the neck from a narrower ribbon of the same colours.

COMMANDEURS wear the decoration round the neck.

OFFICIERS and CHEVALIERS wear the decoration on the left breast from a still narrower ribbon, the former having a rosette in the centre of the ribbon.

THE STAR consists of ten alternate rays of gold and silver, having in its centre a five-rayed star of white enamel, with, between the two upper rays, the Sultan's crown in gold. In the centre, on azure enamel, is an Egyptian inscription meaning:—" What benefits Egypt owes to the Nile, her source of prosperity and happiness ! "

THE DECORATION is similar to the star, but smaller, being suspended from its ribbon by means of a crown.

The various grades of the Order are conferred upon naval and military officers according to their rank, and upon civil officials according to their salaries. Thus, the 4th class cannot be awarded to a civil official whose salary is less than £360 a year.

---

2. VICTORIA CROSS (page 23).—Recipients of the V.C. who have been awarded bars for subsequent acts of gallantry wear on the ribbon, when it alone is worn in undress uniform, the miniature replicas of the Cross in bronze ; one or more according to the number of bars awarded.

9. D.S.O. (page 28).—Companions of the D.S.O. may be awarded bars for further meritorious or distinguished services, and when the ribbon alone is worn in undress uniform they wear on the ribbon a small silver rose ; one or more according to the number of bars awarded.

13. DISTINGUISHED SERVICE CROSS (page 32).—Bars may be awarded to recipients of the D.S.C. in the same way as with the D.S.O. (*vide* above), while the same regulations are in force as to the wearing of the silver rose on the ribbon in undress uniform.

13. CONSPICUOUS GALLANTRY MEDAL (page 32).

14. DISTINGUISHED SERVICE MEDAL (page 33).—Bars may be awarded for subsequent acts of gallantry, and the same regulations obtain as to the wearing of the silver rose on the ribbon in undress uniform as is the case with the D.S.O. (*vide* above).

15. MILITARY CROSS (page 33).—Recipients are entitled to use the letters "M.C." after their names. Bars may be awarded for further meritorious or distinguished services, and when the ribbon alone is worn in undress uniform those who have received bars wear on the ribbon a small silver rose ; one or more according to the number of bars awarded.

16. D.C.M. (page 33).—Recipients of the D.C.M. who have been awarded bars, wear on the ribbon, when it alone is worn in undress uniform, a small silver rose ; one or more, according to the number of bars awarded.

16a. MILITARY MEDAL (page 34).—Recipients of the Military Medal who have been awarded bars, wear on the ribbon, when it alone is worn in undress uniform, a small silver rose ; one or more according to the number of bars awarded.

ADDITIONAL FOREIGN ORDERS WHICH HAVE BEEN CONFERRED UPON BRITISH SUBJECTS.

Country.	Order.	Colour of Ribbon.	Remarks.
BELGIUM	CROWN OF BELGIUM	Purple-brown. Rather similar to No. 117.	Established in 1897. Five classes.
ITALY	ST. MAURICE AND ST. LAZARUS	Bright green watered silk.	Founded in 1434. Five classes.
,,	CROWN OF ITALY	Scarlet watered silk with a broad, white central stripe. Rather similar to No. 64.	Founded in 1868. Five classes.
,,	Medal for Saving Life at Sea	Bright blue with two narrow white stripes towards either edge.	Founded in 1836. Three classes: gold, silver, bronze.
RUSSIA	ST. ANNE	Scarlet watered silk with thin yellow stripe towards either edge.	Founded in 1735. Three classes; but members of a 4th class wear the decoration attached to their swords, while those of a 5th class wear a medal.
,,	ST. VLADIMIR	Scarlet watered silk with broad black edges.	Founded in 1732. Four classes.
SERBIA	WHITE EAGLE	Scarlet watered silk with broad pale blue stripe towards either edge.	Founded in 1883. Five classes.
,,	ST. SAVA	White watered silk with broad light blue stripe towards either edge.	,, ,,
,,	STAR OF KARA GEORGE	Scarlet watered silk with broad white edges.	,, 1904. Four Classes.

ADDITIONAL LIST OF BRITISH DECORATIONS AND MEDALS

Medal or Decoration.	Ribbon.	Remarks.
Queen Victoria's Household Faithful Service.	A peculiar tartan striped pattern about ⅜ in. wide.	
Hong Kong Plague, 1894.	Vermilion, yellow edges, two yellow lines.	Awarded by community of Hong Kong to about 600 officers and men of R.N., Shropshire L.I., and R.E., also to certain nursing sisters and civilians who volunteered to fight the plague which broke out in 1894. Officers received gold medals without ribbons or attachments, and N.C.Os. silver medals with both. An unofficial medal which is not allowed to be worn in uniform.
Kimberley Star 1900.	Half black, half pale ˋ yellow, with broad red, white, and blue stripe down centre.	An ornamental six-pointed star presented by the Mayor of the town to all who took part in its defence. An unofficial medal which is not allowed to be worn in uniform.
British N. Borneo.	Orange watered silk.	Medals were issued by the British N. Borneo Company to all those who took part in punitive expeditions in their territories between 1897 and 1900. Twenty-five silver medals were issued to British officers, and 227 bronze medals to N.C.Os. and men

Medal or Decoration.	Ribbon.	Remarks.
		between these dates. The bronze medals were all exchanged for silver ones in 1906. The medal bears on one side the arms of the British N. Borneo Company, and on the other a lion standing in front of a bush with the Union Flag, charged with the Company's crest, behind. Round the top circumference the words, "British North Borneo," and in the exergue a small wreath and the name of the maker, "Spink & Son, London." Method of suspension the same as No. 85, India General Service Medal, 1908. A bar inscribed "PUNITIVE EXPEDITION" was issued with each medal. The silver medals were originally issued to officers, and the bronze to the rank and file, Indians or Dyaks. War Office sanction was given for the medal to be worn in uniform.
British Red Cross Society's Medal for Balkan War, 1912–13.	White with narrow red stripe down the centre.	Awarded by the Society to nurses and others of its Ambulance Corps who served with the belligerent armies during the war.
Rocket Apparatus Long Service Medal.	Sky blue watered silk with broad scarlet edges.	An official medal established in 1911 and awarded by Board of Trade for long service with the Rocket Life Saving Apparatus. Obverse bears the effigy of the King with legend and date of institution, and the reverse an inscription. It hangs from its ribbon by a scroll clasp.

Medal or Decoration.	Ribbon.	Remarks.
Queen Alexandra's Imperial Military Nursing Service.	Scarlet. Two white stripes towards either edge and two broader dark blue stripes towards the centre.	A decoration conferred upon nurses of these Services who have certain qualifications.
Ditto, Reserve.	Dark blue. Two white stripes towards either edge and two broader scarlet stripes towards the centre.	
Territorial Nurses.	Narrow scarlet ribbon with central narrow white stripe.	A decoration won by certain nurses of the Territorial Force.

INDEX

The figure in black type gives the reference to the coloured representation of the Ribbon, pp. 1–12: other references are to the letterpress, pp. 13–82.

The spelling of names in all instances is that assigned to the respective Medals or Bars as officially issued.

Dates are given where necessary for distinction.

PRINTED BY GEORGE PHILIP & SON, LTD., LONDON.

PLATE I

KING'S COLOUR—1st SCOTS GUARDS

REGIMENTS AT A GLANCE

BY

E. E. DORLING, M.A., F.S.A.

Illustrated with 4 Coloured Plates
and 138 Regimental Badges

LONDON

GEORGE PHILIP & SON, Limited, 32, Fleet Street

Liverpool : PHILIP, SON & NEPHEW, Ltd., 20, Church Street

1917

COLOURED PLATES
AND CONTENTS

3

4

REGIMENTS AT A GLANCE

TO OUR READERS

" WHAT'S he in ? " It is the commonest of questions when every other man one meets is a soldier in khaki. We all want to know something about our soldiers and their regiments. We all have some one near and very dear who is doing his bit ; and in days when every one of us feels a kind of reflected glory in our nearness to our own soldier, and a passionate pride in the doings of all who are playing a man's part in the great game of war, it is a natural and a healthy curiosity that prompts the question.

A considerate government has been careful to distinguish each soldier by devices, such as letters or words upon his shoulder-straps and a badge on his cap, so that anyone may see at a glance in what branch of the service he is. But the natural modesty of the English forbids us to peer closely at the soldier whose identity we wish to discover ; and being a tongue-tied race we shrink shyly from asking a man bluntly what is his regiment.

Some of the badges that our soldiers wear tell the story plainly enough. We all know, for instance, that a man with a little brass image of a field-gun on his cap is in the Royal Artillery. We can trust the instinct which assures us that he who shows crossed lances is a lancer, or that a thistle implies that he is in some corps raised north of the Tweed. But there or thereabouts the military lore of most civilians ceases. There seems to be such an endless variety of regimental badges, and we meet with so many of them every day. What are they all? What do they mean? What is their history?

It is the aim of this little book to tell you. We will show you that some regiments have more than one badge; that in many cases the badge that is fixed in a man's cap is different from that which he wears on the collar of his tunic, different again from the emblem emblazoned on the colour of his regiment. We will tell you something of the history and the significance of those honourable distinctions, how and where they were won, why and where they are borne. We will, in fact, take you a little way into that amazing tale of glory and heroism, the history of the British Army.

Badges and titles which appear upon the clothing and accoutrements of the soldier are also displayed upon the colours of regiments.

Every battalion of infantry in the regular army (except those of rifle regiments) possesses two colours, the King's and the regimental colour, each measuring 45 by 36 inches.

The King's colour of all battalions of Foot Guards is of crimson silk embroidered with the regiment's devices, badges and battle honours, new labels suitably inscribed being added from time to time as fresh honours are conferred by the sovereign; but the regimental title does not appear.

It will be seen from our first illustration (Plate I., frontispiece) that the King's colour of the 1st Scots Guards, for instance, has in the middle a shield of the arms of Scotland with the motto *En! ferus hostis*, surmounted by an imperial crown and flanked by gold labels bearing honours. Below is the Egyptian sphinx in a laurel wreath, given in commemoration of service in Egypt in 1801.

The regimental colour of each battalion of Foot Guards is the Great Union, also bearing badges and honours but similarly omitting the title.

For infantry of the Line the rule is different. The King's colour is the Union flag charged with title and crown, and in some cases with the badge; it is the regimental colour only which shows the honours. In the case of royal regiments the latter colour is of blue silk ; for non-royal regiments the silk is of the same colour as the facings, but when these are white or scarlet the flag is of white silk charged with the red cross of St. George.

Our second illustration (Plate II., facing p. 32) shows the Union which is the King's colour of the Royal Welsh Fusiliers. Here the central cross is emblazoned with the former number of the regiment surmounted by a crown. This is a relatively old colour. In all colours presented since 1900 the regimental title is substituted for the obsolete number.

Regimental colours of the earlier fashion may be recognised from the fact that they have a small Union in the upper corner nearest to the head of the pike. This use has been abandoned in recent years.

The third picture (Plate III., facing p. 64) represents a regimental colour of the Cheshires. Their badge of a slip of oak appears on a golden star in the middle of the red cross, the device, surrounded by the title and placed within a union wreath of roses, thistles and shamrocks, being ensigned with a crown. The honours are inscribed on golden ribbons entwined about two branches of laurel which pass behind the arms of the cross.

In the fourth drawing (Plate IV., facing p. 96) a regimental colour of the Royal Irish is illustrated. The blue silk ground is charged with the regiment's badge of a crowned harp placed upon a crimson roundel, which is edged with gold and inscribed in golden letters with the title. Above is the imperial crown ; and the whole is encircled by a union wreath between laurels on which the honours are shown on gold ribbons. Below are the sphinx for Egyptian service in 1801, and the dragon of China won by the old 18th Foot in the first Chinese war of 1840–42. In each of the four corners is set an escutcheon, in its proper heraldic colours, of the arms of Orange-Nassau with the motto *Virtutis Namurcensis præmium*, a distinction conferred on the 18th as a special mark of favour by King

7

William III. for their magnificent valour at the taking of Namur in 1695.

Those regiments which have simple territorial titles and are not entitled to display royal or ancient badges place the battalion number on the red roundel in the middle.

It should be added that regiments possessing such badges place their battalion numbers in the upper corner of their regimental colour near to the pike head. Our illustrations omit these numbers, because they aim at showing arrangement, colour and form rather than actual representations of typical colours.

The black-and-white drawings in the following pages likewise omit very minute details, such, for instance, as the battle honours on the crosses of Rifle regiments, which are too small to be seen without close examination. It is hoped, however, that their simple, unshaded outlines indicate the general appearance and shape of these ornaments with sufficient clearness to enable our readers to recognise the badge of any regiment in the regular army at a glance.

ROYAL FLYING CORPS

was developed from the Balloon Company of the Royal Engineers, and constituted as a separate entity in 1913 with its present title.

The cap badge consists of the initials R.F.C. crowned in a wreath of laurel. Qualified pilots of the corps wear the badge with the addition of two outspread wings on the left breast of the tunic.

Though the youngest of the fighting services of the Empire, the Flying Corps has already earned a most illustrious reputation. Its motto "*Per ardua ad astra*" very happily describes the nature and the splendour of its achievements.

1st LIFE GUARDS

claim descent from a corps of cavaliers formed by Charles II. in 1660 in Holland, commanded by Charles Lord Gerard, with the title of " His Majesty's Own Troop of Life Guards of Horse." They received their present designation in 1788.

With their brethren of the 2nd Life Guards and the Blues, they were at Dettingen, at Waterloo, at Tel-el-Kebir, and in French's great cavalry dash that relieved Kimberley ; and their fight to a finish in the trenches at Zanvoorde on 30th October, 1914, was described by an eyewitness as one of the finest feats of the war.

The cap badge is the cypher of the sovereign in a circular band inscribed with the regimental title and having a crown above it.

2nd LIFE GUARDS

are the modern representatives of a regiment of horse raised by Charles II. in 1660 as " the Duke of Albemarle's Troop of Guards," which was renamed ten years later " the Queen's Troop of Life Guards," and was numbered " the 2nd Life Guards " in 1788.

The brilliant capture by this regiment of the village of Zwarteleen, on 6th November, 1914, dismounted and at the point of the bayonet, is an achievement of which the 2nd Life Guards may be justly proud.

The cap badge is similar to that of the 1st Life Guards, the word " Second " being on the circular band in place of " First."

ROYAL HORSE GUARDS (THE BLUES)

are the only cavalry regiment in the British Army that can trace its history to the Parliamentary army that fought against Charles I. They were not disbanded, but were added to the establishment after the Restoration, and named in 1690 " the Oxford Blues," from the colour of their uniform and their colonel, Aubrey Earl of Oxford.

The Blues shared in the glory gained by the Household Cavalry at the capture of Zwartelen and Hill 60 on 6th November, 1914, losing their colonel and four other officers, but saving by their steadfast devotion a situation fraught with danger to the British force before Ypres.

Their cap badge differs from that of the other regiments of Household Cavalry only in having " Royal Horse Guards " on the circular band.

1st (KING'S) DRAGOON GUARDS

The first six regiments of Dragoon Guards were raised by James II. at his accession to the throne in 1685, the 1st being entitled " the Queen's Regiment of Horse." Their name was changed to " the King's Regiment of Horse " in 1714, and in 1746 George II. conferred its present title upon the regiment.

Within a few years of its formation the regiment saw service in Flanders, being with William III. at the siege of Namur. It fought under Marlborough in his victories of Schellenberg, Blenheim, Ramillies, Oudenarde, and Malplaquet; under Prince Ferdinand of Brunswick at Warburg; and under Wellington at Waterloo.

The regimental badge is the cypher of the sovereign within the garter. The cap badge is an eight-pointed star, crowned, with the letters $\frac{K}{DG}$ in a disk surrounded by a garter in the centre. The use of the imperial eagle of Austria, formerly worn by the K.D.G. on their collars and caps, has been abandoned since the late Emperor Francis Joseph, colonel-in-chief from 1896 to 1914, was removed from the command of the regiment.

2nd DRAGOON GUARDS (QUEEN'S BAYS)

named "the Queen's Own Royal Regiment of Horse" in 1727 by George II. in honour of Queen Caroline, were converted into dragoon guards in 1746, receiving at the same date their title of "Queen's Bays" from the colour of their chargers.

The tenacity and resource shown by the Bays in the action at Néry on 31st August, 1914, were only equalled by the fighting qualities of the other British troops engaged in that remarkable action, in which three regiments of cavalry and a single battery of Horse Artillery in an inferior position held and, on the arrival of aid, beat off six regiments of German horse supported by twelve guns.

The badge of the regiment is the cypher of Queen Caroline within the garter, and their motto is *Pro rege et patria*. The badge worn upon collar and cap consists of the word BAYS within a crowned laurel wreath.

3rd (PRINCE OF WALES'S) DRAGOON GUARDS

received their present title from George III. in 1746, together with their badges of the Prince of Wales's feathers, the red dragon of Wales, and the rising sun, an ancient device of Edward the Black Prince. The Prince of Wales's feathers is worn by officers and men upon their collars. Their cap badge is the same device with the regimental number on a scroll below.

Their battle honours include Marlborough's four great victories, and "Talavera," "Albuhera," and "Vittoria" in the Peninsula, as well as the (for cavalry) unique honour of "Abyssinia." It is safe to say that the 15th German Army Corps will long remember its encounter with the 3rd D. G. on 17th November, 1914, near Zillebeke.

4th (ROYAL IRISH) DRAGOON GUARDS

named "Arran's Cuirassiers" in 1697 from their colonel Charles Earl of Arran, received their present number and title in 1788 in commemoration of many years' service in Ireland.

The 4th D. G., who are the only Irish regiment of dragoon guards, took part in the charge of the Heavy Brigade at Balaclava; and they have the honour of being the first British troops to come to blows with the enemy in the present war.

They carry on their standard the Irish devices of the crowned harp and the star of the order of St. Patrick, the same star crowned being worn as the regimental badge on head-dress and collar.

5th (PRINCESS CHARLOTTE OF WALES'S) DRAGOON GUARDS

formerly known as "the Green Horse" from their dark green facings, were made dragoon guards in 1788 and received their badge of the white horse of Hanover and their present title in 1804, for their services in the Irish rebellion of 1798.

They saw much hard service under Marlborough and in the Peninsular War, and were in the charge of the Heavy Brigade at Balaclava. Their magnificent shooting at Néry on 31st August, 1914, helped materially to break the attack of the German 1st Cavalry Brigade, and finally to rout the enemy's horsemen.

The regimental motto, *Vestigia nulla retrorsum*, placed upon a crowned circular band, surrounds a disk charged with a galloping horse and the initials $\frac{V}{DG}$, the combination constituting the device which forms the cap and collar badge.

6th DRAGOON GUARDS (CARABINIERS)

entitled when raised in 1685 " the Queen Dowager's Cuirassiers," were renamed " the King's Carabiniers " by William III. in 1691, and received their present title in 1788.

They were in Marlborough's four victories ; and rendered eminent service in the Indian Mutiny. The extraordinary gallantry of Sergt.-Major Wright and Trooper Meston, of the Carabiniers, during the defence of Messines, on 30th and 31st October, 1914, will ever be an inspiration to this famous regiment.

Two of the weapons with which the troopers were originally armed are shown in the regimental badge, crossed behind a crowned garter surrounding the initials $\frac{VI}{DG}$.

The Carabineers are the only regiment of dragoon guards who wear blue tunics, the colour having been changed from scarlet to blue in 1851.

7th (PRINCESS ROYAL'S) DRAGOON GUARDS

were raised by William III. in 1688, being named successively " the Earl of Devonshire's " from their first commander ; " Schomberg's Horse " after their next colonel, Frederick Duke of Schomberg; and "Ligonier's Horse" in 1742 from the distinguished general, John (afterwards Earl) Ligonier, who was colonel of the regiment and raised it to a remarkable state of efficiency of which it gave solid proof at Dettingen. In 1788, George III. conferred the present title in honour of his eldest daughter, and since that date the Princess Royal for the time being has been colonel-in-chief of the regiment, which displays the coronet of the princess in its standard as its principal badge.

The cap and collar badges of the 7th D. G. are the crest of Lord Ligonier, a demi-lion coming out of a coronet, with the title below.

Their nickname of " the Black Horse " is derived from the colour of their facings.

1st (**ROYAL**) **DRAGOONS**

have a very long history, having been raised in 1661 to form part of the garrison of Tangier which had become a possession of the English crown as part of the dowry of Catherine of Braganza, the consort of Charles II. They were transferred to the English establishment as " the Royal Regiment of Dragoons " in 1684, and numbered "the 1st (Royal) Dragoons" in 1751.

At Dettingen they showed eminent valour, breaking the Black Musketeers, and taking their standard.

The cap badge of this famous regiment is the crest of the King, a crowned lion of England standing upon a crown with the name on a scroll below. The collar badge is a representation of the eagle of the French 105th regiment, captured by Captain Clark Kennedy of " the Royals " at Waterloo, when they took part in the famous charge of the Union Brigade. The regimental motto is *Spectemur agendo*.

2nd DRAGOONS (ROYAL SCOTS GREYS)

have always been a Scottish regiment. They are found on the Scotch establishment in 1681, having been raised a few years before that date, and since 1700 have always been mounted on grey horses. They were known by various titles, all testifying to their Scottish origin, till they were numbered the 2nd Royal North British Dragoons in 1866. In 1877 they received their present title.

Their badges are a thistle inside a circular band inscribed with the motto of the order of the Thistle, *Nemo me impune lacessit*, and a grenade. That worn upon the service cap is a representation of the eagle of the 45th French regiment of infantry which Sergeant Ewart of the Greys captured at Waterloo. Their proud motto is *Second to None*.

The nickname of " the Birdcatchers " applied to the Greys, as well as to the Royals, commemorates their exploits at Waterloo ; but characteristic as it is one feels that it scarcely does justice to their brilliancy.

They won the privilege of wearing the grenadiers' bearskin cap, a distinction now enjoyed by no other British cavalry regiment, at Ramillies, where they broke the French Régiment du Roi and captured its standard. The generous praise with which Sir Colin Campbell greeted the " Gallant Greys " when they returned from their ride with the Heavies into the Russian horse at Balaclava is a treasured memory of this magnificent regiment.

3rd (KING'S OWN) HUSSARS

raised as " the Queen Consort's Regiment of Dragoons " in 1685 by James II., received the title of " the King's Own Dragoons " in 1714 from George I. It was not until 1861 that they became hussars.

This regiment under Colonel Bland achieved great distinction at Dettingen, where it lost half its effectives ; and in after-years it shared in the glories won by the British cavalry in the Sikh wars. In the present war the 3rd Hussars highly distinguished themselves in the terrific fighting at Zandvoorde before Ypres on 30th October, 1914.

Their badge is the galloping horse of Hanover with a scroll below inscribed with the regimental number and title.

4th (QUEEN'S OWN) HUSSARS

were raised in 1685 as " the Princess Anne of Denmark's Dragoons," and continued to be heavy cavalry until the end of the wars against Napoleon. They were made into light dragoons in 1818, becoming hussars in 1861 with their present title. The regiment took part in the charge of the Light Brigade at Balaclava, and besides that battle honour has those of " Alma," " Inkerman " and " Sevastopol." They are gaining new laurels in the present war, their work at the canal bridge at Hollebeke on 30th October, 1914, when Sergt. Seddons won the D.C.M., being specially notable.

They bear as a badge the number IV in a crowned band inscribed with their name, with the regimental motto, *Mente et manu*, on a scroll below it.

5th (ROYAL IRISH) LANCERS

descend from a regiment of heavy cavalry formed by William III. in 1689, and named " the Royal Irish Dragoons " from its long service in Ireland. They were present at Marlborough's four great victories, winning great honour at Blenheim and at Ramillies, where they shattered the French Grenadiers de Picardie, and gained the privilege (since taken away) of wearing the grenadier head-dress.

They were disbanded in 1798, but were re-embodied in 1858 with their present title.

The regimental badge is the crowned Irish harp, with the motto *Quis separabit ;* the harp and crown being worn on the collar. The cap badge is their number 5, in a circular band inscribed with the motto, placed in front of two crossed lances.

6th (INNISKILLING) DRAGOONS

raised by William III. in 1689, have throughout their existence been connected with the north of Ireland, although it was not until 1751 that they received their present title. They with the Royals and the Scots Greys formed "the Union Brigade" at Waterloo, and they took part in the charge of the Heavy Brigade at Balaclava.

Their badge is the castle of Inniskilling with St. George's flag flying from the central tower, and the word "Inniskilling" on a scroll below.

7th (QUEEN'S OWN) HUSSARS

were originally a Scottish regiment of heavy horse, being embodied in 1689 as " Cunningham's Dragoons " when trouble was threatening in Ireland. They were at Namur and at Dettingen, and in 1805 were made a hussar regiment with their present number and title in honour of Queen Charlotte. At Waterloo they formed part of Grant's 3rd Brigade on the right of the second line of the Allies.

Their badge consists of the monogram Q.O. reversed and interlaced within a crowned circular band inscribed with the regimental number and title.

8th (KING'S ROYAL IRISH) HUSSARS

were raised in Ireland in 1693. They were employed in Spain in the War of the Spanish Succession, suffering at the defeat of Almanza in 1707, but earning great fame at Saragossa three years later, where for their exploits against the Spanish cavalry they gained the privilege of wearing their sword-belts over the shoulder, together with the nickname of " the Cross Belts." At the beginning of the next century they were in India, and under Lake in the Mahratta War won their motto *Pristinæ virtutis memores* for their gallantry at Leswaree. They were numbered " the 8th " in 1822, and fifty-one years later shared in the glory of the charge of the Light Brigade at Balaclava.

The regimental badge is the crowned harp of Ireland with the title on a ribbon below.

9th (QUEEN'S ROYAL) LANCERS

date their origin from 1697, though the regiment was disbanded shortly afterwards. They were reformed as " Wynne's Dragoons " in 1715 and remained in Ireland until the Peninsular War. They became lancers in 1820 and ten years later were numbered and named with their present title by William IV. in honour of his consort, Queen Adelaide, whose cypher within the garter was given to them as a badge.

The cap badge consists of the number 9 in front of a pair of crossed lances, with a crown above and " Lancers " on a ribbon below the number.

The 9th got their nickname of " the Delhi Spearmen " from the terrible toll which they took of the rebels at the siege of Delhi. That the spirit of the regiment is as high as ever they abundantly proved at Andregnies on 23rd August; at Moncel on 7th September; as well as in the trenches at Messines on 30th and 31st October, 1914, when Corporal Seaton of this regiment won the V.C. for his gallantry in remaining alone in his trench and working a Maxim to cover the retirement of the 1st and 2nd Cavalry Brigades.

10th (PRINCE OF WALES'S OWN ROYAL) HUSSARS

formed by William III. in 1697 were disbanded after the Peace of Ryswick in the same year. They were raised again in 1715, and fought in the Seven Years' War as the 10th Dragoons, earning their first battle honour at Warburg. Before the end of the century they had become " the Prince of Wales's Light Dragoons " with the Prince of Wales as their colonel, and after much hard service in the Peninsula they were in 1811 named " Royal," and made into hussars.

They possess the Welsh badges of the Prince's feathers, the rising sun, and the red dragon, the first-named with a ribbon below it inscribed " 10th Royal Hussars " being used as the cap badge.

The regiment derives its nickname of " the Chainy Tenth " from the peculiar pattern of the pouch belt worn with the full uniform. If " the Tenth don't dance " they have shown the Germans that they can shoot, as they proved at Zillebeke on 17th November, 1914, when, with the 3rd Dragoon Guards, they utterly crushed the final attack of the enemy.

29

11th (PRINCE ALBERT'S OWN) HUSSARS

have an early history corresponding with that of the 9th Lancers and the 10th Hussars. Like the latter regiment they were at Warburg, in the Peninsula, and at Waterloo, and they were in the Light Brigade at Balaclava.

Their machine-gun work, and their charge in the action at Néry on 31st August, 1914, were not the least stirring and splendid of the feats which destroyed the German plans in that astonishing battle.

They were honoured by Queen Victoria with their present title in 1840 on the occasion of their forming the escort of Prince Albert when he landed at Dover ; and the regiment received the badge, which they still bear, of the crest and motto of the Prince.

The 11th Hussars are the only regiment in the service to wear crimson overalls, from which peculiarity they derive their nicknames of "the Cherubims," and "the Cherry Pickers." There is no truth in the legend that they owe the latter nickname to having been surprised somewhere in the Peninsula when raiding a cherry orchard.

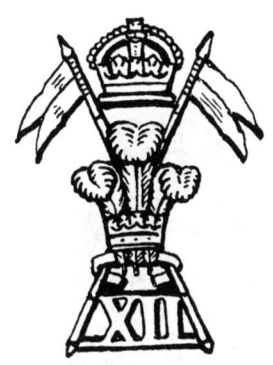

12th (PRINCE OF WALES'S ROYAL) LANCERS

are the descendants of a regiment of dragoons raised just before, and disbanded immediately after, the Peace of Ryswick, but revived in 1715 when the Young Pretender was threatening the Hanoverian dynasty. After being stationed for more than three-quarters of a century in Ireland they went to the Peninsula, and, if the regimental tradition may be believed, were until recently expiating by the nightly playing of certain sacred music an offence there committed against Holy Church. The 12th received their present title in 1817. They were called from India when the Crimean War broke out, and landing on the Red Sea coast marched thence overland to Alexandria as the shortest way to the seat of war, thus gaining their badge of the sphinx. At the close of the Crimean campaign they returned to India in time to do good service under Sir Hugh Rose (afterwards Lord Strathnairn) in the Central Provinces.

The cap badge consists of the Prince of Wales's feathers in front of two crossed lances with a crown above and the number XII below the feathers. The rising sun of the Black Prince and the red dragon of Wales are also borne upon the appointments of the 12th.

In the present war the 12th Lancers have never failed to distinguish themselves. The memory of the bayonet charge which a section of them, led by 2nd Lieut. Williams of the Scots Greys, made at the recapture of Wytschate on 2nd November, 1914, will live long in regimental history.

13th HUSSARS

are an ancient and distinguished corps which belongs to the group of dragoon regiments raised in 1697. After being disbanded, they were re-embodied as light dragoons in 1715. They saw much fighting in the Peninsula, where they were known as " the Evergreens " from the colour of their facings, and " the Ragged Brigade " because of the state to which they were reduced after being engaged in no less than thirty-two actions. They were at Waterloo, and in all the engagements in the Crimea including the charge of the Light Brigade at Balaclava.

The 13th became hussars in 1861, and have for their badge the number XIII, in a crowned and laurel-encircled band inscribed with the motto *Viret in æternum*, with the word " Hussars " on a tablet below.

PLATE II

KING'S COLOUR—ROYAL WELSH FUSILIERS

14th (KING'S) HUSSARS

are the sixth and last of the dragoon regiments formed in 1697, disbanded after Ryswick and re-embodied in 1715. In 1798 they received the title of " the Duchess of York's Light Dragoons," the honorary colonel of the regiment being Frederica, Princess Royal of Prussia, the wife of Frederick Duke of York, commander-in-chief of the British Army. They were renamed the 14th (King's) Hussars in 1861.

They won great fame in the Peninsula, and there too they earned their nickname of " the Emperor's Chambermaids." For after the battle of Vittoria the 14th Light Dragoons found, to their triumphant amusement, in the captured equipment of King Joseph, the Emperor Napoleon's brother, a utensil of solid silver, not to be mentioned to ears polite, but destined thenceforth to be a most jealously treasured piece of the regimental plate.

The badge of the Prussian eagle which was given to the 14th in memory of the Duchess of York is no longer used. That now worn by all ranks is the King's crest in a garter with the title on a ribbon below.

B

15th (THE KING'S) HUSSARS

were formed in 1759 during the Seven Years' War by Colonel George Augustus Eliott (afterwards created Lord Heathfield for his defence of Gibraltar), and were styled " Eliott's Light Horse " after him. The regiment, young and untried, was sent at once to Germany, and for its distinguished conduct at Emsdorff on 16th July, 1760, where it defeated and took five battalions of French infantry with their colours and nine guns, was made " Royal " with the title of " the King's Light Dragoons." It was numbered and named with its present designation in 1806, redeeming the gallant promise of its motto —*Merebimur*— in the Peninsula and at Waterloo.

The stirring exploit of two troops of this regiment on 26th August, 1915, at Bergues, when during the retreat from Le Cateau, they saved the sorely tried remnant of the Munsters, is one which neither regiment will ever forget.

The 15th bear as their badge the King's crest in a garter with their initials XV. K.H. and a scroll inscribed with their motto below.

16th (THE QUEEN'S) LANCERS

raised at the same time as the 15th Hussars as light dragoons, became a lancer regiment in 1816 with the title of "the Queen's" in honour of Queen Charlotte.

After serving with distinction in the Seven Years' War they fought in the Peninsula and at Waterloo, and were afterwards engaged in the Afghan and the Sikh Wars. The "Scarlet Lancers," as they are called, because they are the only lancers to wear scarlet tunics, were the first British regiment to take the field armed with lances.

The regimental badge is the initial C of Queen Charlotte in a garter, and their motto is *Aut cursu aut cominus armis.* The badge worn on cap and collar consists of the number 16 in front of two crossed lances, with a crown above, and the title "the Queen's Lancers" on a scroll below the number.

17th (DUKE OF CAMBRIDGE'S OWN) LANCERS

were raised in 1759 as light dragoons, and almost immediately received the nickname of "the Death or Glory Boys" on account of their well-known badge which their commander, Colonel Hale, had obtained permission for them to wear in memory of his old companion-in-arms General Wolfe. They were converted into lancers in 1816, and saw their first war service in the Crimea, being engaged at the Alma, at Balaclava, where they charged with the Light Brigade, and at Inkerman. In 1876 they received their present title in honour of George Duke of Cambridge, commander-in-chief of the British Army.

18th (QUEEN MARY'S OWN) HUSSARS

were formed in 1759 by Charles sixth Earl (afterwards created Marquess) of Drogheda, and known as " Drogheda's Light Horse." They were in the Peninsula and at Waterloo, and after the Peace of Paris were disbanded in 1821. In 1858 the regiment was formed again as hussars, but saw no war service till the South African war of 1899–1902, in which it formed part of the army defending Ladysmith. It received its present title in 1910, and proved its appreciation of the honour by the way in which it handled the Germans of the 1st Guard Dragoons at Moncel on 7th September, 1914.

Its badge consists of the regimental number XVIII placed upon an H inside a crowned circular band inscribed with the words " Queen Mary's Own," and clasped by two branches of laurel. The motto is *Pro rege, pro lege, pro patria conamur.*

19th (QUEEN ALEXANDRA'S OWN ROYAL) HUSSARS

descend from the 19th Light Dragoons who were raised in 1759 and made into hussars in 1807, having already taken part in the storming of Seringapatam in 1792, and won their badge of the elephant at Assaye in 1803. Sent next to America they saw the end of the War of Independence, being the only cavalry regiment in the service with the honour " Niagara." Subsequently the 19th served with distinction in Egypt in the campaigns of 1882 to 1885.

Their badge is the crowned initial A of Queen Alexandra, their colonel-in-chief, interlaced with the cross of Denmark inscribed with the date 1885. The elephant is worn upon the pouch belts.

20th **HUSSARS**

were raised originally in 1759, and disbanded four years later. Formed once more in Ireland in 1789 they fought in the Peninsula, and again were disbanded after Napoleon's fall. They were embodied for the third time in India in 1860, when they received their present number, and have twice been campaigning in Africa. In the present war they rendered good service in the retreat from Mons and again before Ypres.

Their badge is a crowned H between two X's.

21st (EMPRESS OF INDIA'S) LANCERS

as at present constituted date from 1858, when they were the 3rd Bengal European Cavalry, but they claim to represent the old 21st Light Dragoons, who were raised in 1760 by John Marquess of Granby. They came on the English establishment in 1862 with the title of " the 21st Hussars," and were changed to lancers in 1897. They won their battle honour of " Khartoum " under Kitchener in 1898, and for their gallant charge at Omdurman were rewarded by Queen Victoria with their present title.

They derive their nickname of " the Grey Lancers " from the colour of their plastron and facings.

Their badge is the crowned imperial cypher, VRI, of Queen Victoria above the regimental number XXI, placed before two crossed lances.

ROYAL REGIMENT OF ARTILLERY

dates as a permanent force from the year following the first Jacobite rebellion, when the old haphazard system of raising artillery trains for each campaign and disbanding them immediately afterwards was abandoned. The Garrison Artillery is the oldest of the three branches into which the regiment is divided, and may be regarded as the modern representatives of a force formed for siege and defence as long ago as the days of the Hundred Years' War. The Field Artillery was formed in 1716, and the Royal Horse Artillery was organised in 1793, when England joined the first coalition against France.

The history of the Royal Artillery is, as has been well said, the history of the British Army, for as the mottoes of the regiment claim, the artillery goes everywhere where duty and glory show the way.

The regimental badges are the royal arms, and a gun between the two mottoes " *Ubique* " and " *Quo Fas et Gloria ducunt*," with a crown above it.

It seems invidious to mention one rather than another of the countless instances in our many wars in which the

41

valour, the skill, and the devotion of British artillerymen have shed fresh glory on their magnificent regiment. But for sheer gallant picturesqueness it would be hard to find in all its history a more superb example of the cool intrepidity which earns its just reward than the fight of L Battery of the Royal Horse Artillery in the orchard at Néry.

Scourged by a torment of German fire at a range of only 400 yards, the battery fought until, with its commander, Captain Bradbury, killed and all the other officers wounded or dead, with only a single gun in action and but four men able to serve it, the survivors, under Sergt.-Major Dorrell, had the satisfaction of firing the last shot in the battle, and that at the retreating foe !

CORPS OF ROYAL ENGINEERS

was formed, like the Royal Artillery, into a military force in 1717, their services in the Highlands having been of immense value during the operations against the forces of the Old Pretender. After being called by various titles they became " the Royal Sappers and Miners " in 1813, and at the end of the Crimean War received their present designation.

Their regimental badge is the royal arms with the mottoes " *Ubique* " and " *Quo Fas et Gloria ducunt.*" On their caps the Royal Engineers wear a device of the cypher of the sovereign in a crowned garter surrounded by a wreath of laurel with the title of the corps inscribed on a scroll.

The aim and the achievements of the Royal Engineers are, as their mottoes proudly declare, like those of the Royal Artillery : they go everywhere, and they can do anything.

GRENADIER GUARDS

formerly " the 1st Foot Guards," were originally raised about 1656 by Thomas Lord Wentworth from the cavaliers who had gathered round Charles II. in the Low Countries. At the Restoration in 1660, the King decreed that " our own Regiment of Foot Guards shall be held and esteemed the oldest regiment." The title of " Grenadier Guards " was given to the regiment after Waterloo where they shattered the Grenadiers of the Old Guard of Napoleon. Their battle honours begin with " Tangier 1680 ; " and their services at the taking of Namur, in Marlborough's victories, at Dettingen, in the Peninsula, in the Crimea and in Africa testify to their fighting qualities.

The badge of the Grenadiers is naturally a grenade which is borne on their caps, their collars and shoulder straps. In full dress they wear a plume of white goat's hair on the left side of their bearskin headdresses.

In the present war the Grenadiers have more than sustained their high reputation. To name only one taken at random of innumerable instances of the unflinching determination of this eminent regiment : at the battle of the Kruiseik cross-roads on 29th October, 1914, the 1st battalion (a unit of the British force of 5,000 men defending Ypres which beat off 24,000 Germans) went into action with 16 officers and 650 men. Before they received orders to retire they had been reduced to 150 rank and file and 4 officers.

COLDSTREAM GUARDS

are the representatives of a force raised in 1650 by the Protector Cromwell, who from two regiments of the New Model Army made a corps which, as "Colonel Monck's Regiment," was commanded by the famous George Monck, afterwards Duke of Albemarle. They soon became "the Lord General's Regiment of Guards," and at the Restoration were incorporated into Charles II.'s army as "the 2nd Foot Guards." Their present title, given in 1817, is a revival of the name by which they were known familiarly when they returned to England after a spell of duty at Coldstream in Berwickshire in Cromwell's time.

Charles II. sent them to Tangier, and they were at Namur in 1695, and at Gibraltar in 1704-5. They won, under Marlborough, the honours of "Oudenarde" and "Malplaquet," and fought under George II.'s eyes at Dettingen. After service in the Peninsula, where they gained great renown they fought at Waterloo. In the Crimea, where their astonishing tenacity at Inkerman won them immortal fame, they shared the glory and the sufferings of the army before Sevastopol, adding later in Egypt and in South Africa to their well-earned honours. Of the noble service of the Coldstream in the present war, no act is finer in its dogged endurance than their holding of the trenches, unrelieved for over three weeks, in the Polygon wood outside Ypres in October and November, 1914.

Their badge is the star of the order of the Garter. Their plume is of scarlet feathers, worn on the right side of the bearskin.

SCOTS GUARDS

were raised in Scotland in Charles I.'s time, and transferred to the English establishment at the Restoration, with the title of " the 3rd Foot Guards." In 1831, William IV. gave them the name of " the Scots Fusilier Guards," and authority to wear the bearskin cap common to the other regiments of Foot Guards. In 1877 they were named " the Scots Guards " by Queen Victoria.

They shared the arduous work of the other regiments of the Household Brigade at Waterloo, and in the Crimea ; as well as in the African campaigns of 1882 to 1902.

A very notable feat was performed by the Scots Guards on 26th October, 1914, when after losing one of the trenches before Kruiseik they recaptured it in a night attack, taking at the same time more than 200 German prisoners.

Their badge is the star of the order of the Thistle, and they wear a thistle on the collars of their tunics. In full dress Scots Guards may be distinguished from the other Foot Guards by the fact that they have no plume in their bearskins.

IRISH GUARDS

embodied in 1901, in token of Queen Victoria's appreciation of the deeds of the Irish in the South African war, are building up a reputation in the present war which adds lustre to the traditions of the Household Brigade.

The regimental badge is the star of the order of St. Patrick, and all ranks have a leaf of shamrock embroidered on the collar. The plume, worn on the right side of the bearskin, is of blue feathers.

WELSH GUARDS

were raised by his present Majesty in 1915, the leading company of the 1st battalion being named "the Prince of Wales's Company."

The badge of the regiment is a leek.

THE ROYAL SCOTS (LOTHIAN REGIMENT)

date their constitution from 1633, having been raised in that year in Scotland by Sir John Hepburn. The regiment was transferred to the English establishment as the 1st of the Line at the Restoration, and was known as "Douglas's Regiment" from its colonel Lord James Douglas. For its services at Tangier it was named "the Royal Regiment," its 2nd battalion being raised in 1684. It received the title of "the 1st (The Royal Scots) Regiment" in 1871, and its present designation in 1881.

The Royal Scots have fought with distinction in almost every part of the world, the only important operations which they have missed being the Indian Mutiny.

Their share in the capture of Orly on 7th September, 1914, and their brilliant seizure of the line of the Lawe Canal in the following month are feats which will ever rank high in the records of the Royal Scots.

The bonnet badge is the star of the order of the Thistle having in the middle the figure of St. Andrew with his cross above a ribbon inscribed with the title; the badge worn on the collar is a thistle.

The strange nickname of "Pontius Pilate's Bodyguard," by which this regiment is known, arises from the fact that in an argument with the French Régiment de Picardie, Douglas's Scots, who had been lent by Charles II. to Louis of France, laid claim to a greater antiquity than that of the French regiment, who affirmed that they had been on guard at the Crucifixion!

THE QUEEN'S (ROYAL WEST SURREY REGIMENT)

was raised as "the Tangier Regiment" in 1661 by Henry Mordaunt, Earl of Peterborough, to garrison the town of Tangier, of which he was governor. Charles II. named it "the Queen's" in honour of his consort, Catherine of Braganza, and from that time it has borne the badge of the Holy Lamb, that device being a favourite badge of the royal house of Portugal. In 1751 it was named "the 2nd (the Queen's Royal) Regiment of Foot," and received its present territorial designation in 1881.

Its ironical nickname of "Kirke's Lambs," which embodies the name of its colonel at Tangier as well as the badge, was given for its fierceness in battle against the Moors; the name became doubly significant from the ferocious treatment of the Somersetshire peasants by this regiment after Monmouth's rebellion in 1685.

The Queen's proved their worth in the Peninsular War, and afterwards in Afghanistan, in China, and in South Africa; and when the 1st and 2nd battalions fought side by side at Gheluvelt on 31st October, 1914, the enemy again learnt something of their indomitable valour. A week later the charge of the Queen's at Zwartelen taught the Germans what they may expect who face the cold steel of the " Mutton Lancers."

A badge, borne on the colour, of which the Queen's are justly proud, is a naval crown conferred, with the date, " 1st June, 1792," for the share they had in Howe's glorious victory over the French fleet off Ushant.

The sea has yielded them another deathless honour. It was a detachment of the Queen's that stood fast and died when the *Birkenhead* went down.

THE BUFFS (EAST KENT REGIMENT)

raised as " the Holland Regiment " for the Dutch service in the wars against Spain, in Queen Elizabeth's days, were brought to England in 1665, and added to the army as " the 3rd Foot." Its title of " the Buffs " was given on account of the buff leather coats formerly worn by the regiment, the colour being retained for its facings after the 3rd had become scarlet-clad. The territorial title, " East Kent," was conferred in 1782.

The regimental badge is the red dragon of the royal house of Tudor. Their nickname of " the Resurrectionists," which some believe to have arisen from the claim of the Buffs to an antiquity as great as that of the Royal Scots, is more probably due to their astonishing recovery after being trampled nearly out of existence by Soult's lancers at Albuhera in 1811. They fought hard throughout the Peninsular War, and did good work in South Africa in 1879 and again in 1900–1902. Their storming of Radinghem on 18th October, 1914, was a feat worthy of the high reputation of this ancient and distinguished regiment.

THE KING'S OWN (ROYAL LANCASTER REGIMENT)

formerly " the 4th Foot," was raised in 1680 as the 2nd Tangier Regiment by Thomas Hickman, Lord Windsor. It was the first considerable body of troops to join William of Orange after his landing at Torbay in 1688, and received its badge of one of the English lions in the royal arms as a special mark of William III.'s favour. George I. in 1715 named it " the King's Own," and the present title of " Royal Lancaster " was conferred in 1881.

Its first foreign service was at the capture of Namur from the French in 1695. This battle honour, which the King's Own shares with the three senior regiments of Foot Guards and ten other infantry regiments, was granted as late as 1910.

Its next honour was won at the siege of Gibraltar, and it did great work in the Peninsula, at Waterloo, and in the Crimea. The King's Own helped to relieve Ladysmith ; and with the Northumberland Fusiliers accomplished a notable feat in the recapture of Le Gheir on 20th October, 1914.

THE NORTHUMBERLAND FUSILIERS

are the descendants of a regiment raised for service in Holland in 1674 when William Prince of Orange was striving desperately against the French. Brought to England in 1688 they were added to the English army as the 5th Foot, receiving their fusilier caps in 1762 for their overthrow of a body of French grenadiers at Wilhelmstahl in Prussia, where also they won their first battle honour. The territorial designation " Northumberland " was granted in 1782, their colonel being Hugh Earl Percy. Their nickname of " the Fighting Fifth " was given for their valour in the Peninsular War, in which campaign they gained no less than twelve honours.

The regimental badge is a representation of St. George and the Dragon, with the motto " *Quo fata vocant* " ; and an interesting custom which is observed in the regiment is that of wearing roses in the headdress on St. George's day. The cap badge is a grenade with the regimental device of the saint upon the ball.

THE ROYAL WARWICKSHIRE REGIMENT

formerly the 6th of the line, had served for several years in Holland before it came back to England with William of Orange in 1688. Seven years later it was once more in the Low Countries and shared in the taking of Namur. It was one of the five English regiments that suffered severely on the bloody field of Almanza, 14th April, 1707; but it took its revenge at Saragossa, three years after that disastrous day, when it captured, with other Spanish flags, one bearing the device of an antelope, which beast was given to the regiment by Queen Anne for a badge in memory of its achievement. A little more than a century later the 6th won high praise from Wellington himself, who characterised their fighting at Echalar in the Pyrenees as " the most gallant and the finest thing he had ever seen." The title " Royal Warwickshire " was given in 1832.

The way in which the 2nd battalion stormed the German position at Reutel on 24th October, 1914, proved that the Warwicks have lost none of their old impetuous valour.

THE ROYAL FUSILIERS (CITY OF LONDON REGIMENT)

date their origin from 1685, when James II. raised a body of foot armed with fusils as an ordnance regiment for the protection of the artillery. Four years later they became " the 7th (Royal Fusilier) Regiment ; " a title retained till 1881, when they lost their number and received the territorial title.

Their battle honours include all the great engagements of the Peninsular and the Crimean Wars. The Royal Fusiliers covered themselves with glory at the battle of Mons, on 23rd August, 1914, where they won two Victoria crosses for their stubborn defence of the salient between the Ghlin and the Nimey bridges.

The cap badge is a rose in a crowned garter placed upon the ball of the grenade which is the distinguishing mark of this as well as of the other eight fusilier regiments of the British Army.

THE KING'S (LIVERPOOL REGIMENT)

was raised in 1685 by James II. For its eminent services in Marlborough's campaigns, Queen Anne named it "the Queen's," a title which George I. altered at his accession in 1715 to its present designation of "the King's." In 1751 it was numbered the 8th of the line. Its connection with Liverpool dates from 1881.

The regimental badge is the white horse of Hanover (conferred by George I. at the renaming of the regiment) within the garter, and the motto is *Nec aspera terrent*. It should be noted that the horse of "the King's" is shown in the attitude of leaping, a posture which distinguishes it from the other horses used as badges in the service.

The cap badge consists of the horse placed upon a scroll inscribed with the title of the regiment.

THE NORFOLK REGIMENT

raised in 1685, won its first battle honours in the West Indies, and saw continuous fighting in the Peninsular War and again in the Sikh War of 1845. It has been connected with the county of its title since 1782, when it was named the 9th (East Norfolk) Regiment of Foot.

Its distinctive badge of the seated figure of Britannia holding a branch of laurel was gained at Almanza in 1707, when a British force, heavily outnumbered by a French and Spanish army under James Duke of Berwick, sustained a decisive defeat. The disaster, severe as it was, would have been far heavier but for the valour of this regiment, which, though almost annihilated in covering the retreat, upheld the honour of Britain and was rewarded by the grant of this most honourable badge. All the Empire was thrilled the other day when we heard how the Sandringham men of the Norfolk Territorials had maintained the regimental tradition in Gallipoli.

The Norfolks have the curious nickname of "the Holy Boys," given to them in the Peninsular War when our Spanish allies mistook the badge of Britannia for a figure of the Virgin Mary.

THE LINCOLNSHIRE REGIMENT

was formed in 1685. It earned great renown in the victories of Marlborough, and again in the Sikh War when the glorious conduct of the regiment at Sobraon was described in general orders as the corner stone of the victory. In 1782 it was named "the 10th (North Lincolnshire) Regiment of Foot," retaining that number and title till 1881, when the present designation was given.

Of the Lincolns' deeds in the present war it would be hard to find any that surpassed in dash and brilliancy the taking of Herlies, in company with the Royal Fusiliers, on 17th October, 1914.

The Lincolns' badge of the sphinx, won at the Atbara and Khartoum in the Egyptian campaign under Kitchener, in 1898, is placed within a circular band inscribed with the title upon an eight-pointed star when worn upon their head-dresses. The collar badge is the sphinx with the name "Egypt."

The nickname of "the Poachers" is an allusion to the old song, "the Lincolnshire Poacher," which is the regimental march of the county regiment.

THE DEVONSHIRE REGIMENT

another of James II.'s regiments, raised in 1685, has covered itself with glory in every country and in every campaign in which it has been engaged. It was entitled " the 11th (North Devonshire) Regiment of Foot " in 1782, and gained its grim nickname of " the Bloody Eleventh " at Salamanca in 1812, where it came out of action with only four officers and sixty-seven rank and file. Among other honours on their colours, the Devons have " Relief of Ladysmith " as well as " Defence of Ladysmith," because the 2nd battalion was in the army under Buller which raised the siege of the town in whose defence the 1st Devonshire played so gallant a part.

But nothing that they have ever done was a greater achievement than their indomitable stand at Givenchy in October, 1914. In those sixteen days the Devons surpassed even themselves.

The badge of the regiment is a representation of the castle of Exeter in a circular band inscribed with the title placed upon a crowned star; and their motto is that of the city— *Semper fidelis.*

THE SUFFOLK REGIMENT

formed in 1685, had already achieved fame at Dettingen
and at Minden before it formed part of the immortal garrison
of Gibraltar in the siege of 1779 to 1783, where it won its badge
of the castle and key. It was named " the 12th (East Suffolk)
Regiment of Foot " in 1782, and on account of its number has
had for many years the nickname of " the Old Dozen."

The cap badge consists of a representation of the castle
of Gibraltar with a key (typifying that that fortress is the key
of the Mediterranean) below the gate and the inscription
" Gibraltar " above it, within a crowned circular band inscribed
" *Montis insignia Calpe* " and flanked by two branches of
oak, with the regimental title on a ribbon at the base of the
design.

PRINCE ALBERT'S (SOMERSET LIGHT INFANTRY)

were formed in 1685, and numbered the 13th Regiment of the Line in 1751, having already won distinction at Gibraltar and Dettingen. In 1842 they were named " the 13th (Somerset-shire) Prince Albert's Light Infantry Regiment," and received with their bugle badge the unique distinction of a mural crown with a scroll inscribed " Jellalabad " for their gallant defence of that town in the first Afghan War of 1839–42. The Government of India gave special thanks to " the illustrious garrison " for that splendid feat of arms ; and the Queen conferred on the regiment the privilege, which the sergeants enjoy, of wearing their sashes over the left shoulder, as, until recently, commissioned officers wore them, because during the five months' siege of the Afghan town, so many of the officers of the 13th were incapacitated that their duty had to be undertaken by the sergeants of the regiment.

THE PRINCE OF WALES'S OWN (WEST YORKSHIRE REGIMENT)

raised in 1685, began its war service at the taking of Namur, ten years later. As the 14th Foot it was at Corunna with Moore, and afterwards at Waterloo ; and it saw service in the New Zealand wars. For many years a Buckinghamshire regiment, the Prince of Wales's Own got their nickname of " Calvert's Entire " from the fact that about 1818 the regiment was largely composed of men recruited on the Buckinghamshire estates of its colonel, General Sir Harry Calvert. A better known nickname is " the Old and Bold."

In 1881 the territorial designation was changed to " West Yorkshire."

The cap badge is the galloping horse of Hanover with the title " West Yorkshire" on a ribbon below. The devices on the regimental colour are the Prince of Wales's feathers, the tiger, for services in India under Lake in 1805, and the white horse with the Hanoverian motto *Nec aspera terrent*.

THE EAST YORKSHIRE REGIMENT

was formed in 1685, being numbered the 15th Foot in 1751, and receiving the territorial designation of " Yorkshire, East Riding " in 1782. It thus has a very long association with the county. It was with Marlborough at his great victories in the Low Countries, and distinguished itself by remarkable work at Blenheim. Half a century later the 15th were with Wolfe at Quebec, winning special praise from the general, in whose memory the officers, to this day, wear two threads of black woven in their gold lace.

The badge is the white rose of York encircled with bays and placed upon an eight-pointed star with the regimental title as a scroll below.

This regiment has the curious nickname of " the Snappers," which tradition says was earned in the American War on an occasion when a party of the 15th, surrounded by rebels and without ammunition, continued to snap their muskets with such determination that the enemy forbore to come to close quarters.

PLATE III

REGIMENTAL COLOUR—CHESHIRE REGIMENT

THE BEDFORDSHIRE REGIMENT

was formerly the 16th Foot. Raised by James II. in 1688, the regiment was connected in its early days with the county of Buckingham ; hence its badge of a buck and its nickname of " the Old Bucks." When in 1809 the 16th was named " the Bedfordshire Regiment " it retained its old Buckingham-shire badge.

It is one of the Namur regiments, and was with Marl-borough in Flanders, taking part in his four great victories of Blenheim, Ramillies, Oudenarde, and Malplaquet. After Dettingen, when the gallantry of the 16th extorted generous praise from the defeated French, many years elapsed before they took the field again, and it is believed that their nick-names of " the Peacemakers " and " the Featherbeds " had their origin during that long period of inactivity.

The cap badge is a Maltese cross charged with a buck crossing a ford and surrounded by a garter, which device with the county name is placed upon a star of eight points.

THE LEICESTERSHIRE REGIMENT

is historically the first of William III.'s regiments, having been raised in 1688. It was at Namur in 1695 and in the wars in America in the next century, where it served under Wolfe. Although it was not at Quebec the regiment (already numbered the 17th Foot and named " the Leicestershire " in 1782) still specially commemorates the death of General Wolfe in that battle by the so-called " worm," a line of black in the gold lace worn by officers.

The brilliant services of the Leicesters in India and Afghanistan in the nineteenth century are symbolised by its badge of the tiger, which is borne on the colours with the superscription " Hindoostan ; " on the collar in a laurel wreath ; and on the cap with the word " Leicestershire " on a scroll below. Their nickname is " the Bengal Tigers."

THE ROYAL IRISH REGIMENT

formerly the 18th Foot, was raised by James II. in 1684 in Ireland from the remains of the Commonwealth army serving there. It remained on the Irish establishment till William III. incorporated it in the English army, and for its valour at Namur gave to the 18th the badges of the crowned harp of Ireland and his own arms of Nassau with the motto *Virtutis Namurcensis Praemium*. Its name " the Royal Irish " was given in 1751.

The regiment was with Marlborough in his victorious campaigns, and has distinguished itself greatly in three Egyptian campaigns, adding thereby the sphinx to its badges. It has suffered terrible losses in the present war, the brilliant capture of Le Pilly by the 2nd battalion on 19th October, 1914, being followed on the next day by the retaking of the place by the Germans and the enforced surrender of what was left of the Royal Irish.

ALEXANDRA, PRINCESS OF WALES'S OWN (YORKSHIRE REGIMENT)

was formerly the 19th Foot, and was raised in 1688 from the Parliamentary veterans of Devonshire. Although present at the taking of Namur, it does not bear that battle-honour, but Malplaquet, the only one of Marlborough's greater victories in which it took part, appears on its colours. The regiment, long territorially connected with the North Riding of Yorkshire, was named "the Princess of Wales's Own" in 1875, and received its present title in 1881. Its ancient nickname, "the Green Howards," is derived from its grass-green facings and the name of its first colonel. The regiment fought through the whole of the South African War, winning special distinction at the Relief of Kimberley and at Paardeberg.

Its badge is Alexandra, Princess of Wales's cypher and coronet combined with a Danish cross inscribed 1875 ; below appear a rose of York, and a scroll with the regimental title.

THE LANCASHIRE FUSILIERS

were raised in 1688 by William III., and as "Kingsley's regiment" won great fame at Minden. After the battle it was announced in an order of the day that the regiment "from its severe loss, will cease to do duty;" but two days later, at its own request, it resumed "its portion of duty in the line." It fought throughout the Peninsular War, earning high praise from Wellington, and was in the Crimea, the Indian Mutiny, and in South Africa, living everywhere up to its proud motto, "*Omnia audax.*"

It was named "the 20th (East Devonshire) Regiment of Foot" in 1782, and received its present title at Childers' reorganisation of the army in 1881.

The badge is a sphinx with the word "Egypt," won at Khartoum in 1898, surrounded by the laurel wreath which had been conferred on "Kingsley's Stand" after Minden. These combined devices are placed upon the ball of a grenade, which has the regimental title on a ribbon placed below it.

THE ROYAL SCOTS FUSILIERS

trace their origin to a regiment armed with fusils which was raised by Charles, 26th Earl of Mar. They were named "the Earl of Mar's Fusiliers" in the Scotch list of 1678, and transferred in 1689 to the English establishment, being numbered later the 21st Foot, with the title of "the Royal North British Fusiliers." In 1877 they received their present designation.

They took part in Marlborough's victories of Blenheim, Ramillies, Oudenarde, and Malplaquet, and earned the special praise of George II. at Dettingen. In the Crimea, in Africa, and in India, this gallant regiment taught its foes the truth of its Scottish motto, "*Nemo me impune lacessit,*" and in the campaign of 1914, proved at Mons, at Illies, and at Gheluvelt that they had lost none of their old power to sting.

Their cap badge is a grenade with the royal arms upon the ball. The collar badge is also a grenade, but the ball is charged with a Scottish thistle.

THE CHESHIRE REGIMENT

was formed by Henry, 7th Duke of Norfolk, in Wiltshire in 1689, during the Irish troubles at the beginning of William III.'s reign, and gained its first battle honour at Louisburg in the Seven Years' War. After performing eminent deeds in the West Indies it was in 1782 named " the 22nd (the Cheshire) Regiment of Foot," and in the next century was part of the tiny British force under Sir Charles Napier which broke the power of the Beloochees at Meeanee and Hyderabad, in the Scinde War of 1843.

The regimental badge of a sprig of oak (placed when worn as a cap badge in an eight-pointed star with the name " Cheshire " on a scroll below) was given by George II. at Dettingen where he had exposed himself so gallantly that he was only saved from capture by the French cavalry through the steadfastness of the 22nd. That the Cheshires have retained that military virtue is plain from their stubborn holding of their part of the Armentières—Givenchy line on the 20th and 21st October, 1914.

THE ROYAL WELSH FUSILIERS

formed by Henry, 4th Lord Herbert of Chirbury, in 1689, have been connected with the Principality from the first. They were numbered the 23rd in 1751, having received their present territorial title in 1714. Their long list of battle honours, from " Namur 1695 " to " Pekin 1900," shows that they have fought in practically every great battle and in nearly every campaign of the British Army ; and the way in which they stood and died before Ypres, at Zonnebeke, at Ledeghem, and at Zandvoorde, in October, 1914, proved for the hundredth time the extraordinary tenacity of this ancient and eminent regiment.

The badges upon their colour are the feathers of the Prince of Wales, the rising sun of the Black Prince, the red dragon of Wales, the white horse of Hanover, and the sphinx for Egypt. Their cap badge is a grenade with the Prince of Wales's feathers, in a circular band inscribed with the regimental title, upon the ball.

The Welsh Fusiliers enjoy a unique and highly prized distinction in the wearing of " the flash," a knot of black ribbons sewn to the back of the collars of their officers' tunics. This represents the patch of black leather which, before the abolition of pigtails in 1808, served to protect the uniform from being soiled by those ornaments, which this regiment is said to have been the last in the army to wear.

THE SOUTH WALES BORDERERS

were formed in 1689, and named in 1782 "the 24th (2nd Warwickshire) Regiment of Foot," receiving their present title in 1881.

They helped to win Marlborough's four great victories, and after serving in the campaign at the Cape of Good Hope in 1806, went on to the Peninsula, where they gained nine battle honours. For their prowess in the Sikh War they received the nickname of "the Bengal Tigers," but they suffered terribly at Chillianwallah, where they were almost entirely destroyed.

The 24th was one of Abercromby's regiments in Egypt in 1801, and they consequently have a sphinx as their badge with the initials S.W.B. below it. The wreath of immortelles and laurels which surrounds it was given for two terrific fights in Zululand, 22nd January, 1879—at Rorke's Drift, where one company under Lieutenants Chard and Bromhead of the Royal Engineers beat off 4000 Zulus, and at Isandlwana, where the rest of the regiment was annihilated. But the Queen's colour was saved by Lieutenants Melville and Coghill, who died in its defence ; and Queen Victoria conferred on both battalions the privilege of bearing a silver wreath on the staff of the colour in memory of that day of glory and sacrifice.

THE KING'S OWN SCOTTISH BORDERERS

raised in 1689 by David, 3rd Earl of Leven, for the defence of Edinburgh, were severely handled by the Highlanders under Claverhouse at Killiecrankie a few months later. They were with William III. at Steinkirke and at the taking of Namur, and gained their next battle honour at Minden, where, as the 25th Foot, they were one of the six immortal regiments which proved the fighting power of the British infantry by the way in which they charged and broke the cavalry of Contades. In this present war they showed at Mons and Le Cateau how they could stand and endure.

The regiment was named " the King's Own Borderers " by George III. in 1805, and received the white horse as one of its badges, having already earned the sphinx under Abercromby at Alexandria in 1801. In 1881 this essentially Lowland regiment was renamed " the King's Own Scottish Borderers."

The bonnet badge consists of a conventional representation of the castle of Edinburgh upon a St. Andrew's cross superimposed on a circular band inscribed with the regimental title and encircled by a wreath of thistles. Below on a ribbon is the motto, " *Nisi Dominus frustra*," and above is the second motto, "*In veritate religionis confido*," the whole surmounted by the King's crest.

74

THE CAMERONIANS (SCOTTISH RIFLES)

are a Lowland regiment, raised in 1688 among the Covenanters, after one of whom, the famous preacher Richard Cameron, they were named. Their first colonel was James Earl of Arran, and in memory of him a molet from his coat of arms is placed above the strings of the bugle in the cap badge of this famous rifle regiment. In 1826 they were numbered the 26th Foot.

The 2nd battalion, formed by Sir Thomas Graham in 1794 as " the 90th (Perthshire Volunteers) Light Infantry," was nicknamed " the Perthshire Grey-Breeks " from the county of their origin and the colour of their breeches. When they were linked with the Cameronians in 1881, the present title was given.

The Cameronians were with Marlborough in Flanders, and with Moore at Corunna ; the Perthshires earned the honour " Sevastopol " in the dreadful winter of 1854, and took part in the first relief of Lucknow, in the Mutiny.

Their badges are the sphinx, which the 90th won in Egypt in 1801, and the dragon, superscribed " China," granted to the 26th for their services in the Chinese War of 1841.

THE ROYAL INNISKILLING FUSILIERS

The 1st battalion, raised in 1689, was named in 1751 " the 27th (Inniskilling) Regiment of Foot," and fought in William III.'s Irish campaigns ; but saw no foreign service till 1762, when it earned the battle honours of " Martinique " and " Havannah." It was in all the hottest fighting in the Peninsula, and showed its mettle at Waterloo and in the South African wars of 1835 and 1846–7, and again in the Mutiny, where it won the honour " Central India." The 2nd battalion, raised in India in 1854, was named " the 108th (Madras Infantry) Regiment " in 1861.

The present title was given when these two battalions were linked together in 1881.

The regimental badges are the white horse of Hanover and the sphinx, with the castle of Inniskilling, the last-named being placed upon the ball of the grenade.

THE GLOUCESTERSHIRE REGIMENT

Both battalions have a long and intimate connection with the county. The 1st, formed in 1694, became the 28th Foot, and in 1782 received the territorial title of " North Gloucestershire ; " the 2nd, raised in 1758, was numbered the 61st Foot in 1782, and designated " the South Gloucestershire."

The regimental badge of a sphinx in a laurel wreath was won by the 28th at Alexandria, 21st March, 1801, when the regiment in line on the right of the British army was suddenly attacked by a strong body of French cavalry. Not having time to form square the Gloucesters, coolly obeying the order, " Rear rank, right about face," fought back to back and beat off their assailants. For this fine feat of arms the regiment enjoys the unique privilege of wearing the badge on the back as well as on the front of the headdress, and earned the nickname of " the Fore and Aft." The 61st were also in Egypt in that campaign, being brought from India. Landing at Kosseir on the Red Sea they marched with the rest of Baird's army to the Nile at Keneh and so down the river to Alexandria.

Both battalions were engaged in the Peninsular War. At Waterloo the 28th fought and died with the same invincible courage as was shown in after-years by the 61st at Chillianwallah. The 28th won the three Crimean honours of "Alma," "Inkerman," and "Sevastopol," and the 61st added "Delhi" to the long roll of thirty-four battle honours which the Gloucestershire Regiment possesses.

THE WORCESTERSHIRE REGIMENT

consists of two west-country corps, the old 29th raised in 1694 and named "the Worcestershire Regiment of Foot" in 1782, and the 36th which was formed in 1701 and entitled "the Herefordshire Regiment" in 1782. To these, linked in 1881 under the present title, two more regular battalions have since been added.

At Ramillies, the only one of Marlborough's four victories in which either battalion was engaged, the 29th earned their first battle honour; but they share the Peninsular honours about equally, the 36th having won a slightly larger number. The 29th, however, brought their score level by their doings in the Sikh War.

The motto of the Worcestershire Regiment is "Firm," and there is no regiment in the service that has a better right to that proud word, as they proved at Gheluvelt on 31st October, 1914, when their work in repelling the furious effort of the Germans to break through to Ypres was characterised by Sir John French as one of the finest achievements in the campaign.

Their badge is an eight-pointed star with the royal crest surrounded by a garter in the middle and the motto *Firm* on a ribbon on the lowest point. Below the star is a scroll inscribed with the regimental title.

Another badge highly prized by the Worcesters is their naval crown, with the date "1st June, 1794," conferred for their share in Howe's naval victory over the French off Ushant.

THE EAST LANCASHIRE REGIMENT

consists of the old 30th Foot, raised in 1702 specially for sea service, and the 59th Foot who were formed in 1755. Neither battalion had anything to do with Lancashire until 1881, the 1st being styled in 1782 " the 30th (Cambridgeshire) Regiment," while the 2nd in the same year was named " the 59th (2nd Nottinghamshire) Regiment."

The 30th were at the taking of Gibraltar in 1704, and a hundred years later the 59th helped to capture the Cape of Good Hope. Both battalions were in the Peninsula, where seven battle honours were won, as well as in the Waterloo campaign, though the 59th did not take part in the great battle itself. In the Crimea the 30th were engaged at the Alma and at Inkerman ; and in 1857 the 59th, at the storming of Canton.

The cap badge is a sphinx inscribed " Egypt," won by the 1st battalion at Alexandria in 1801, above a rose of Lancaster, the whole surrounded by a crowned laurel wreath, with the title on a ribbon below. A Lancaster rose is worn as the collar badge.

THE EAST SURREY REGIMENT

The 1st battalion is the old 31st Foot, raised for service at sea in 1702, and named " the Huntingdonshire Regiment " in 1782. They were at the taking of Gibraltar and at Dettingen, and in the fiercest battles of the Peninsula. Afterwards in the East they were at the reoccupation of Cabool in 1842, and in the Sikh wars. The 2nd battalion, raised in 1758, was later numbered the 70th Foot, and having received the title of " the Surrey Regiment " in 1825, served with distinction in New Zealand between 1860 and 1869.

The nickname of " the Young Buffs " dates from the battle of Dettingen, where George II., admiring the gallantry of the 31st, but misled by their facings, exclaimed, " Well done, Old Buffs ! " Being told that he had mistaken the regiment, the king cried, " Well done, then, Young Buffs ! "

The regimental badge of the East Surrey consists of a shield of the arms of Guildford, the county town, ensigned with a crown and set upon an eight-pointed star, with the title on a scroll below.

THE DUKE OF CORNWALL'S LIGHT INFANTRY

is composed of the old 32nd Foot (raised in 1702 and named
" the Cornwall Light Infantry " in 1858), and the 46th Regiment (which dates from 1741, and was named " the South
Devonshire " in 1782).

The 1st battalion began its career at the taking of Gibraltar
under Sir Cloudesley Shovel, and served with great distinction
in the Peninsula and at Waterloo. The 2nd battalion treated
the Americans so severely at Brandywine in 1777 that the
angry rebels vowed to give them no quarter when next they
met. Whereupon the Englishmen dyed the feathers of their
hats red that they might be recognised, and so earned their
nickname of " the Red Feathers," their gallant bravado being
symbolised by the little piece of red cloth that is still worn
behind the cap badge. The 32nd earned undying fame in the
Mutiny for their eighty-seven days' defence of the Residency
at Lucknow. When they were linked with the 46th in 1881,
the present title was given.

The cap badge is a bugle with the coronet of the Duke of
Cornwall above the strings and the word " Cornwall " on a
scroll placed across them.

The shield of arms of the Duchy appears in the collar badge ;
it is ensigned with the coronet and placed upon a sixfoil
inscribed with the Cornish motto, " One and all."

THE DUKE OF WELLINGTON'S (WEST RIDING REGIMENT)

is the only regiment in the British Army associated with the name of a person not of royal birth, and the only red-coated infantry corps which has scarlet facings.

The 1st battalion was raised in 1702, being eventually numbered the 33rd Foot. It received the territorial designation "1st Yorkshire, West Riding, Regiment" in 1781; and in 1853 was named "the Duke of Wellington's Regiment" in honour of the recently deceased commander-in-chief who had served in it as a major, and in 1806 became its colonel.

The 2nd battalion, formed in 1782 as the 76th Foot, also bears on its roll of officers the name of the Iron Duke, for he served in it for a few weeks as Lieut. Arthur Wesley. Both battalions fought under him in India, the 33rd distinguishing itself at Seringapatam, and the 76th winning great honour at Leswarree. The 33rd again came under the Duke's command at Waterloo; and in the Crimea won the honours of "Alma," "Inkerman," and "Sevastopol."

The cap badge is the crest of the Duke of Wellington, a demi-lion coming out of a crown and holding a flag, with the motto of the Wellesleys, "*Virtutis fortuna comes.*" Another highly prized badge which recalls the Indian service of both battalions is an elephant with a howdah on its back, superscribed "Hindoostan."

THE BORDER REGIMENT

so named in 1881, consists of two battalions long associated with the extreme north-west of England. The 1st, raised in 1702, after service in the West Indies became in 1782 " the 34th (Cumberland) Regiment." It afterwards fought in the Peninsula, where it gained, with many other distinctions, the unique honour of " Arroyo dos Molinos " for capturing the 34th French infantry of the line, whose drums are still a prized possession of the battalion. For this achievement the Cumberlands enjoyed for many years the privilege of wearing the red and white pompons in their headgear with the red uppermost, in the French fashion.

The 2nd battalion, formerly the 55th Foot, was raised in 1755. It was named " the Westmoreland Regiment " in 1782, and won the badge of the dragon for its services in the first Chinese War. The Westmorelands were at the Alma and at Inkerman, and met their Cumberland neighbours before Sevastopol. Their invincible fortitude for six terrible days in the last week of October, 1914, in the trenches at the Zandvoorde road, will always be an inspiration to this gallant regiment.

The honours of the two battalions are combined in the badge, a Maltese cross with a lion between each division surrounded by a wreath. A circle in the centre of the cross has upon it the inscription " Arroyo dos Molinos 1811," enclosing a dragon and the word " China."

THE ROYAL SUSSEX REGIMENT

was raised at Belfast in 1701 as the 35th Foot and gained its badge of the " Rousillon Plume " in 1759, when it captured the standard of the Rousillon Grenadiers at Quebec. When Malta was taken in 1801, the King's colour of the 35th Foot was the first English flag to be raised on Fort Ricasoli. The nickname of the " Orange Lilies " dates from the time when the regiment wore orange facings, and was known as the " Prince of Orange's Own."

The 2nd Battalion, formerly the 107th Bengal Infantry Regiment, traces its origin to the Queen's Own Royal British Volunteers, first raised in 1760, but re-formed in 1854.

The Royal Sussex shared in the glory of the victory at Troyon on 14th September, 1914, losing more than a fourth of their strength in that encounter.

The regimental badge is the star of the order of the Garter, behind which is a single upright ostrich feather—the " Rousillon Plume." But the more distinctive collar badge retains the plume and substitutes for the star a Maltese cross ensigned with a laurel wreath in memory of the taking of Malta. Within the wreath is the garter enclosing the cross of St. George.

THE HAMPSHIRE REGIMENT

The 1st battalion, raised in 1702, and named later the 37th (North Hampshire) Regiment of Foot, was one of the six British regiments which won undying fame at Minden, and the rose in the Hampshires' badge commemorates their share in the astonishing charge that wrecked the French cavalry on that glorious day. As they marched to the field of battle some of the men had plucked roses in the gardens of the little village and stuck them in their headdresses, and as a reminder of the great achievement that followed the Hampshire Regiment has the privilege of wearing roses on the anniversary of the victory.

The 2nd battalion, formed in 1756 with the title of the 67th Foot, to which the territorial designation of " South Hampshire " was afterwards added, won the tiger badge for its twenty-one years' service in India after the Peninsular War. " The Hampshire Tigers " is naturally the nickname of this distinguished regiment; and the regimental badge, consisting of a tiger above a rose, is thus a happy combination of devices which tell of famous events in the history of the two battalions of the regiment.

The cap badge of the Hampshires is a union rose within a crowned garter above a ribbon inscribed with the title, the whole set on an eight-pointed star.

THE SOUTH STAFFORDSHIRE REGIMENT

consists of the 38th (1st Staffordshire) Regiment of Foot, which was formed in 1702, and the 80th (Staffordshire Volunteers) Regiment of Foot, raised in 1793, and thus has always been connected with the county whose name it bears.

The 38th, after spending the first fifty and odd years of its existence in the West Indies, where it earned the honours " Guadaloupe 1759 " and " Martinique 1762," was sent to North America, where it fought at Bunker Hill ; thence to the Cape of Good Hope, and from there to South America, where it lost an idolised commander, Colonel Vassall, and gained the honour " Monte Video " in an almost forgotten and disastrous expedition. The Peninsula and India, the Crimea and the Mutiny, Egypt and South Africa have all added to the glory of the South Staffords. The 2nd Battalion (the 80th) numbered Lord Wolseley among its subalterns, and served under him in Egypt, as it had done under Abercromby, when it suffered shipwreck both on the way to Egypt and on the way back to India. The same ill-luck attended it also on its way from Australia to India in 1844.

The South Staffords are a great shooting regiment, as the Germans learned to their cost at the Zonnebeke road on 21st October, 1914.

The colour badge, a sphinx with the inscription " Egypt," is not so distinctive as the " Stafford Knot," which was in ancient days the heraldic badge of the barons of Stafford, and now, surmounted by a crown, forms the cap badge of the regiment.

THE DORSETSHIRE REGIMENT

consists of the 39th Foot, raised in 1702, and the 54th Foot (West Norfolk), raised in 1755.

The 39th was the first King's regiment to serve in India, as its motto " *Primus in Indis* " records. At Plassey in 1754, it won its first honour, as well as the drum major's staff still treasured by the 1st battalion, which was presented to the 39th for valour by the Nawab of Arcot. This was not its first service, for it had fought at Almanza in 1707, when the union flag of England and Scotland first flew in action. There the 39th earned the nickname of " Sankey's Horse," from their hasty arrival on the field mounted on mules.

It had also distinguished itself in the defence of Gibraltar both in 1727 and under Eliott in 1779–82.

The 2nd battalion (the " Flamers ") have a fiery and amphibious record, having gained their nickname from their share in the burning of twelve privateers and the town of New London (U.S.) in 1781, and the warm commendation of the C.-in-C. for their gallantry on board the burning troopship *Sarah Sands*. Their fine work in Egypt in 1801 gave them their badge of a sphinx with the unique inscription " Marabout," which surmounts, within a wreath of laurel charged with the county name, the castle and key of Gibraltar and the " *Primus in Indis* " of the 40th, to form the regimental badge of the Dorsets.

The regimental nickname " the Green Linnets " arises from the colour of the facings.

THE PRINCE OF WALES'S VOLUNTEERS (SOUTH LANCASHIRE REGIMENT)

is formed of the old 40th (2nd Somersetshire), and 82nd (Prince of Wales's Volunteers). The former was raised in Nova Scotia and Newfoundland in 1717, and its earlier honours were won in the western hemisphere, in 46 years of service. The 40th also fought throughout the Peninsular War, gaining a long list of honours thereby. The honour " Niagara " comes strangely between " Peninsula " and " Waterloo," and records a brief but strenuous period of service in the birth-continent of the 40th.

It was Abercromby's landing at Aboukir which gave them their badge of a sphinx.

The 82nd was raised in 1793, and served in the Walcheren Expedition.

The badge consists of the sphinx of the 40th surmounted by the Prince of Wales's plume of the 82nd, the two within a wreath inscribed " South Lancashire, Prince of Wales's Vols."

The nickname " The Excellers " is of course derived from the XL of the 40th, to whom also belongs the fine title of the " Fighting Fortieth."

THE WELSH REGIMENT

The first battalion was first raised as a regiment of old soldiers for home duty, and was known as " the 1st Invalids," becoming the 41st (The Welsh) Regiment of Foot in 1822. The 2nd battalion is the old 69th, which was formed in 1756, and received the territorial name of " South Lincolnshires " in 1782.

The 69th owe to Nelson their nickname of " Old Agamemnons " from the ship in which they served under him as marines at St. Vincent. They also saw sea service under Rodney, and earned their badge of a naval crown for their part in the victory over de Grasse on 12th April, 1782. Their honours range from the West Indies to " South Africa," and include " Waterloo," " India " and the Crimean battles.

Another nickname of the 69th is the " Ups and Downs," from the fact that their numeral reads the same either way up.

The cap badge is the Prince of Wales's plume with the name of the regiment below on a ribbon.

THE BLACK WATCH (ROYAL HIGHLANDERS)

consists of the 42nd, raised in 1729, and the 73rd, raised in 1780.

It is the senior Highland regiment, beginning its splendid record at Fontenoy, with the same valour that has distinguished it ever since, and has earned it a long list of honours. On that field, one man, who had slain nine of the enemy, was in the act of cutting down the tenth when a shot carried away his arm. The first eleven years of its existence, however, were spent in the work of keeping peace in the Highlands, and it was not until 1740 that it was enrolled as a British regiment. Its dark tartan, which gives it the name of the " Black Watch," is due to the amalgamation of many tartans by the elimination of all the light-coloured stripes. Its red hackle is a reward for bravery at Geldermalsen in the Flanders campaign of 1795, in which Wellington first smelt powder. After this war " Troyon " will surely be added to its honours.

The bonnet badge of the " Forty-Twas " is a star of the order of the Thistle, whereon is a crowned disk charged with the figure of St. Andrew within the Scottish motto and encircled by a wreath of thistles, with the addition of the name of the regiment, and of the sphinx with the inscription " Egypt."

THE OXFORDSHIRE AND BUCKINGHAMSHIRE LIGHT INFANTRY

In 1741 was raised the 43rd (Monmouthshire Light Infantry) Regiment, and in 1755 the 52nd (Oxfordshire Light Infantry) Regiment, now the first and second battalion respectively of the Oxford and Bucks LI.

The united honours of the two battalions form a magnificent list, both battalions having done splendid service in the Peninsula, for which they, with the Rifle Brigade, had been well prepared by their training under Sir John Moore at Shorncliffe. " Waterloo " is among their honours; but one that is as well deserved but is not borne upon the colour is the " Birkenhead."

In the present war they won immortal fame for their share in crushing the attack of the Prussian Guard before Ypres on 11th November, 1914.

Their nickname the " Light Bobs " is a reference to their formation as light infantry,

The badge worn on the headdress is the light infantry bugle; that borne upon the colour is the united red and white rose.

THE ESSEX REGIMENT

is formed of the old 44th and 56th, which were raised in 1741 and 1755 as the East and West Essex Regiments respectively.

The regiment earned honours in Cuba, the Peninsula, and at Waterloo. At Salamanca the 44th captured the eagle of the 62nd French regiment of the line, and was the first to plant its colours on the walls of Badajoz. In 1841 the whole of the 44th perished in the Khyber Pass, Dr. Brydon alone reaching Jellalabad to tell the tale.

The " Two Fours," or " Little Fighting Fours " as they are variously known, have more obviously derived nicknames than the 56th, whose name " The Pompadours " and " Saucy Pompeys " is derived from the old colour of their facings, a dull crimson much affected by Madame de Pompadour, and named after her. The 56th served in the long siege of Gibraltar ; hence the cap badge combines the castle and key of Gibraltar with the sphinx and " Egypt " within a wreath of oak leaves inscribed " The Essex Regt." The collar badge however is a shield of the arms of the county, three " seaxes " or Saxon knives.

THE SHERWOOD FORESTERS (NOTTINGHAM-SHIRE AND DERBYSHIRE REGIMENT)

The 1st battalion was raised in 1741 and numbered the 45th Regiment of Foot ten years later. Since 1787 when the name of "the Nottinghamshire (Sherwood Foresters) Regiment" was conferred, it has been connected with the county of its title. It fought in Spain throughout the six years of the Peninsular War, and earned its nickname of "the Old Stubborns" for its unconquerable valour at Talavera. In 1881 it was linked with its neighbours of the next county, the 95th (Derbyshire) Regiment, which had been formed in 1823.

The Sherwood Foresters greatly distinguished themselves in the battle of the Aisne, showing remarkable dash and initiative on the very first day of their arrival at the front.

A deer lying down (from the arms of the town of Derby) and surrounded by a wreath of oak typifying the Notts forest of Sherwood is the central emblem of the badge of the regiment, which bears these appropriate devices upon a crowned Maltese cross charged with ribbons upon which the regimental title is inscribed.

93

THE LOYAL NORTH LANCASHIRE REGIMENT

is composed of the 47th (Lancashire) Regiment of Foot, and the 81st (Loyal Lincolnshire Volunteers) Regiment of Foot, deriving its unique epithet from the latter. The 47th was raised in 1740, in Scotland, and served under Sir John Cope (the " Johnny Cope " of the derisive Jacobite song, to whose strains the 92nd (Gordons) took Arroyo dos Molinos). Known as " Wolfe's Own " from its share in his Canadian campaign, it was at the taking of Quebec, and a black line in the lace of the officers commemorates his death.

The 81st did fine work in the Indian Mutiny, being at Meean Meer when it broke out.

The regiment is the only one bearing the honour " Defence of Kimberley." Their capture of the Sugar Factory at Troyon on 14th September, 1914, has been described as one of the finest achievements of the present war.

Their cap badge is the rose of Lancaster surmounted by the royal crest, and over a scroll with the words " Loyal North Lancashire." Possibly the nickname "the Cauliflowers " is a reference to the heraldic form of the rose in the badge.

The collar badge refers to the original title of the 2nd battalion, being the arms of the city of Lincoln, a fleur-de-lis on a cross.

94

THE NORTHAMPTONSHIRE REGIMENT

is composed of the 48th (Northamptonshire) and the 58th (Rutlandshire) Regiments of Foot, which were raised in 1741 and 1755 respectively.

Both battalions have a fine record and fought side by side many times before being linked into one. The 48th fought at Culloden before the 58th had come into being, and it is to the heroism of the senior battalion at Talavera that the regiment owes that honour, which is shown upon the badge. The 58th contribute the rest of the badge, which consists of a wreath with ribbons above and below inscribed with the words "Gibraltar" and "Talavera," and enclosing the castle and key won by the Rutlandshire Regiment in Eliott's defence of the Rock. The name of the county upon a scroll below completes the cap badge. The collar badge is a crowned circle inscribed with the name of the regiment and enclosing St. George's cross with a horseshoe beneath it in reference to the famous horseshoes at Oakham Castle in Rutlandshire.

The Northamptons suffered terrible losses in the Ypres woods during the immortal stand of the 7th Division; but they got something of their own back on the afternoon of 2nd November, 1914, when their tenacity and their superb musketry contributed largely to the foiling of the enemy's attempt to hack a way through to Calais.

The nickname "The Steelbacks" was earned by the 48th in the bad old days of flogging, from the way the men took their punishment. A more honourable title, "the Heroes of Talavera" and yet another, "the Black Cuffs," speak for themselves.

PRINCESS CHARLOTTE OF WALES'S (ROYAL BERKSHIRE REGIMENT)

is made up of the 49th, raised in 1743 and formerly called the Hertfordshire (Princess of Wales's) Regiment, and of the 66th (Berkshire) Regiment formed in 1758.

Their fine record justifies their nickname of " the Brave Boys of Berks." The 49th fought at Copenhagen as marines, and earned honours in the Crimea. The 66th lost their colours at Maiwand, but won undying glory in the loss. The regiment continues to uphold its great traditions in the present war. It accomplished a very fine performance at the Zonnebeke road on 24th October, 1914, when the gallantry and tenacity of the Berkshires were of the utmost value in the operations before Ypres.

The title " Royal " was won at Tofrek in the Sudan in 1885. The dragon badge, despite the reference to Wales in the title of the regiment, is not a Welsh dragon, but Chinese, and is a record of the service of the 49th in the far East. A scroll with the name " Royal Berkshire " completes the badge.

PLATE IV

REGIMENTAL COLOUR—ROYAL IRISH REGIMENT

THE QUEEN'S OWN (ROYAL WEST KENT REGIMENT)

is formed from the 50th and the 97th, raised in 1755 and in 1824 respectively.

The former has a long roll of Peninsular honours, winning its strange nickname of the " Dirty Half Hundred " by its exploit at Vimiera, when the men of the 35th, their faces black with powder and smeared with sweat, swept down upon Laborde's 5000 French and routed them. At Corunna they earned the praise of Sir John Moore, " Well done, 50th, well done ! "

The title " West Kent " was soon given to the regiment. Till 1831 the officers wore black velvet facings, and when in 1831 the regiment became royal, the colour was changed to blue, but the privilege of wearing velvet was retained.

The 97th were known as the " Celestials " from their sky-blue facings. They are of Irish origin, and were first known as " the Earl of Ulster's Regiment."

Neuve Chapelle is a name that will for ever be prized in the records of the Royal West Kents, who for three days held a corner of the town against overwhelming odds, with the loss of over 300 men and of all their officers but two.

The regimental badge of a rearing horse with the proud motto " *Invicta* " is familiar to all as the sign of the county of Kent, which is honoured in giving its name to this brave regiment.

Other nicknames are " the Blind Half Hundred," from the prevalence of ophthalmia in the regiment at one time, and " the Devil's Royals " from their fierce impetuosity in attack.

THE KING'S OWN (YORKSHIRE LIGHT INFANTRY)

consists of the 51st Foot, raised in 1756, and the 105th (Madras L.I.), which was formed in 1839 as an East India Company regiment and never came to England till 1874. Thus the Peninsular honours were gained by the 1st battalion which has always been a Yorkshire corps, its title from 1821 being 2nd Yorkshire (West Riding) King's Own Light Infantry.

The 105th has a good record of Indian service, which gives its Eastern honours to the regiment. In the present war, the K.O.Y.L.I. have earned undying honour, from the moment when by the death of Lieut. Pepys of the machine-gun section at the battle of Mons the 2nd battalion earned the melancholy distinction of losing the first man killed in action in the 5th division. In the terrible day of Le Cateau the same battalion won two V.C.'s and lost 20 officers and 600 men, Major Yate charging the entire German attack with the last 19 men of B company, who had held on to the last minute, and died fighting to a man.

The badge of this splendid regiment is a French horn encircling the white rose of York.

The nickname the " Kolis " is of course taken from the initials of the regiment, and has an appropriate sound-reference to the coal miners of the West Riding, among whom the regiment is largely recruited. It is a curious fact that the present initials K.O.Y.L.I. exactly reproduce the dialect pronunciation of the word " coalie," by which the miners are commonly known.

THE KING'S (SHROPSHIRE LIGHT INFANTRY)

The 1st battalion was raised in 1755, and in 1782 was numbered the 53rd (Shropshire) Regiment, winning nine years later the unique honour of " Nieuport " for its defence of the Belgian town against the French. It bore its full share of the fierce fighting in the Sikh War, where it won the distinctions of " Aliwal," " Sobraon," and " Goojerat," together with the general honour of " Punjaub."

The 2nd battalion, formed in 1793, was originally named " the Bucks Volunteers " and numbered the 85th. It was in the Peninsular War from 1811 to 1814, taking part in most of the engagements of those crowded years, and received its bugle with the title of " the King's Light Infantry " in 1821.

The regimental nicknames of " the Young Bucks " and " the Brickdusts " refer respectively to the original home of the 2nd battalion, and the red facings formerly worn by the 1st.

A bugle with the initials K.S.L.I. under the strings is the cap badge of the regiment.

THE DUKE OF CAMBRIDGE'S OWN (MIDDLESEX REGIMENT)

is formed of the 57th (West Middlesex), raised in 1755, and the 77th (East Middlesex), Duke of Cambridge's Own, raised in 1787.

The 57th earned its honourable name, " the Die-Hards " at Albuhera, where 22 officers out of 25 were killed or wounded, and of 570 other ranks, 425. The memory of Albuhera carried the regiment to victory at Inkerman ; and at Croix Barbée in the present war the men of Middlesex proved that they can still die hard.

The 77th was among the regiments that stormed the breach at Ciudad Rodrigo, and has a fine record of service to its credit, though its nickname, the " Pothooks " is only a reference to its numeral.

The Middlesex is essentially a London regiment, and has amply proved the fighting value of the city dweller. It has four battalions.

Its badge consists of the cipher and coronet of George Duke of Cambridge surmounted by the Prince of Wales's plume. No regiment in the service has a clearer right to the wreath of laurel enclosing them, which has at the foot a scroll inscribed " Albuhera." The name of the regiment on a ribbon below completes the design.

THE KING'S ROYAL RIFLE CORPS

This valiant corps was raised in America in 1755, when it numbered many Swiss in its ranks. Until 1824 it was known as the 60th (Royal American) Regiment of Foot. It became a rifle regiment in 1797 and its scarlet uniform was changed to green with scarlet facings, being the first green-coated regiment of rifles in the service. In 1830 it gained its present title of the King's Royal Rifle Corps, though it is still very commonly known as " the 60th."

It has the longest list of honours in the British Army, all of which are crowded in the manner of Rifle regiments, who carry no colours, upon the cap badge, a simple black Maltese cross surmounted by a crown and a tablet bearing the appropriate motto, *Celer et Audax*. In the centre of the cross is a circle inscribed with the name of the corps and enclosing a stringed bugle. No collar badge is worn.

The nicknames " Greenjackets " and " Sweeps " both refer to the dark green colour of the full-dress uniform, which at a little distance appears black. It is said that the corps has recently been named " the Kaiser's Own " from a fancied resemblance of the badge to the Iron Cross.

THE DUKE OF EDINBURGH'S (WILTSHIRE REGIMENT)

is made up of the 62nd (Wiltshire), who were raised in 1756 as a 2nd battalion of the King's Own, and formed into a separate regiment two years later, and the 99th, raised in 1824, and afterwards designated the Duke of Edinburgh's Lancashire.

The 62nd fought in the American War of Independence, where it earned the nickname of the "Springers" from the eagerness of its pursuit of the rebels after the fight at Trois Rivières. It has also the rare distinction of having gained a nickname from fighting within the British Isles, for at the siege of Carrickfergus, having run short of bullets, the men fired their buttons away. For this they were awarded the honour of wearing a "splash" of lead in their buttons, and so got the name of "the Splashers."

The nickname of the "Moonrakers" is a reminder of the craftiness of the Wiltshire peasant, certain of whom are said to have explained their attempts to secure contraband goods hidden in a duckpond, by pointing to the reflection of the moon and declaring that they were trying "to rake thic cheese" out of the water.

The honour "New Zealand" records the share of the 99th in the trying Maori wars of 1849–1869.

The badge is a cross formy surmounted by the coronet of a royal duke and having in the centre a convex circular plate bearing the cypher of Alfred Duke of Edinburgh.

THE MANCHESTER REGIMENT

The old 63rd Foot, raised in 1756 as a 2nd battalion of the 8th Foot, and receiving its numerical precedence as a distinct regiment in 1758, became known in 1782 as the West Suffolk Regiment. The 96th Regiment of Foot was raised in 1824, and seems never to have had a territorial title. These are the parent regiments of the Manchester, which worthily maintains the record of its predecessors. The re-taking of Rue du Marais, and the splendid defence of Festubert in October, 1914, which earned for the regiment two Victoria Crosses, are still fresh in memory.

The significant nickname of the regiment is "the Bloodsuckers." A regimental badge is the sphinx on a tablet inscribed "Egypt;" that worn on cap and collar is the elaborate coat-of-arms of the city of Manchester, with supporters, an antelope and a lion wearing a civic crown, the crest of a globe, and the name "Manchester" on a ribbon below. This should not be confused (as it often is) with the General Service badge, which consists of the royal arms, crest, and supporters.

THE PRINCE OF WALES'S (NORTH STAFFORD-SHIRE REGIMENT)

The 64th (2nd Staffordshire) Regiment of Foot, raised in 1756 to be a 2nd battalion of the 11th Foot but given a separate status in 1758, and the 98th, formed in 1824, make up this regiment.

The 64th were with Havelock when he avenged Cawnpore and brought the first relief to Lucknow. The short Persian campaign of 1856 had already given them the honours "Reshire," "Bushire," "Khoosh-ab," and "Persia," which they share only with the Durham Light Infantry. The 98th received its title of "Prince of Wales's," on the occasion of the Prince's visit to Malta in 1876.

The nickname "the Black Knots" is a variant, derived from the black facings of the 64th, of the nickname of the South Staffords.

The cap badge is the Stafford knot surmounted by the Prince of Wales's plume and set upon a ribbon inscribed "North Staffordshire." In the collar badge the ribbon is omitted.

THE YORK AND LANCASTER REGIMENT

The 1st battalion was formed in 1756 as the 65th Foot and named the 2nd Yorkshire (North Riding) Regiment soon afterwards. It put in more than twenty years' service in India after its arrival there in 1803, and then was transferred to Australia and New Zealand, staying in the Antipodes for another two decades. The 2nd battalion, formerly the 84th Foot, was raised two years later than the 1st, and received the territorial designation of " the York and Lancaster " in 1809. It also has a notable Indian record, many of the regiment being destroyed in the massacre of the garrison of Cawnpore in 1857, while the remainder formed part of the little force that defended Lucknow. This battalion won great glory on 18th October, 1914, for its share in the capture of Radinghem and its gallant pursuit of the flying Germans ; but it lost in those operations 400 men and eleven of its officers.

The cap badge consists of the Indian tiger with the coronetted rose of York and Lancaster above him and surrounded by a laurel wreath on which is a scroll inscribed with the regimental title. The tiger and rose are worn as the collar badge.

THE DURHAM LIGHT INFANTRY

The 1st battalion was raised by a Lambton in 1756 to serve as the 2nd battalion of the Royal Welsh Fusiliers; but in 1812 after valiant service in the Peninsula, it was transferred to the north of England as the 68th Durham Light Infantry.

The 2nd battalion, raised by the East India Company in 1826, as the 2nd Bombay European Regiment, and renamed in 1840 the 106th Bombay Light Infantry, was in the Persian campaign of 1856–57, and had the little-known honours of " Persia," " Reshire," " Bushire," and " Koosh-ab," when it made its first visit to England in 1871, only ten years before it was linked with the 68th. The present war has proved them, as ever, " the Faithful Durhams."

The bugle, which is their cap badge, has a crown above, and the initials D.L.I. below the strings.

THE HIGHLAND LIGHT INFANTRY

The splendid record of this regiment is equally shared by the
71st and 74th, its parent regiments. The former was raised
in 1777 as Fraser's Highlanders, becoming known later as
Macleod's Highlanders, after John Lord Macleod to whom
the warrant for raising the regiment was issued. The 71st
originally had two battalions of which the 2nd began its
career as marines with Rodney, and served at St. Vincent.
The 1st battalion of the 71st gained Indian honours in 1781–
91. The 71st and 74th share the long list of honours in the
Peninsula, where the former earned the nickname of the
" Glesca' Kilties " from the number of Glasgow men in its
ranks. They became light infantry in 1809 and took part
in the final assault at Waterloo.

The 74th was raised by Sir Archibald Campbell in 1787,
and in 1803, in company with the 78th, won the honour
" Assaye" and the elephant, and their nickname of " the
Assayes," in the first battle with Wellesley in command.

After its magnificent part in repelling the attack of the
Prussian Guard, on 11th November, 1914, General Willcocks
concluded his address to the battalion with the memorable
words, " There is no position which the Highland Light
Infantry cannot capture."

The nickname, " the Pig and Whistle Light Infantry,"
refers irreverently to the badge, which consists of a star of
the Thistle charged with a French horn ensigned with a crown.
Within the circle of the bugle is the monogram H.L.I., and
below it the elephant of the 74th surmounted by a ribbon
inscribed " Assaye."

SEAFORTH HIGHLANDERS (ROSS-SHIRE BUFFS, THE DUKE OF ALBANY'S)

The 72nd Highlanders, first raised in 1756 as "Fraser's High-landers," were disbanded in 1763, to be re-formed in 1778. In the early years of the 19th century the regiment abandoned the kilt, to which, however, it reverted before long. The 2nd battalion, raised in 1756 as the 2nd Highland Battalion, was re-formed in 1793 as the 78th Highlanders (Ross-shire Buffs).

The Clan Mackenzie supplied the greater number of the recruits at the re-institution of the 72nd, and the tartan of the regiment is that of this clan.

The splendid record of the Seaforths is largely Asiatic, the less widely distributed honours of "Persia," "Peiwar Kotal," and "Charasiah" being among them. The Egyptian record is especially fine, Tel-el-Kebir and the Atbara especially being memorable in the regimental history.

A nickname of the 72nd is "the Macraes" from the number of men of that clan in the regiment. The 78th are "the King's Men," a nickname derived from the motto "Cuidich'n Righ" (Help to the King) of the Mackenzies, which is shown in the bonnet badge below the stag's head of Mackenzie, Earl of Seaforth. Between the antlers is placed the coronetted initial L of Leopold Duke of Albany. Another badge motto is "Caber Feidh" (the Antlers of the Deer), the war-cry of the Mackenzie clan; it appears in the collar badge on a ribbon below the initial F of Frederick Duke of York and Albany. The elephant badge for Indian service is also a collar badge of the regiment.

THE GORDON HIGHLANDERS

The 1st battalion, known at various periods as the 75th Foot and the " Stirlingshire," was raised in 1787 among the clansmen of Alexander Duke of Gordon, whose son George Marquess of Huntly became colonel of the regiment in 1796. If the story is true that the beautiful Duchess of Gordon promised a kiss to each recruit, there is probably something in the tradition that the regiment was raised in record time. The 2nd battalion, numbered as the 92nd Highlanders, was formed in 1794, being then known as the 100th (Gordon Highlanders) Regiment of Foot.

There is hardly a campaign of the British Army, as there is scarcely a quarter of the globe, in which one or other of the battalions of this famous regiment has not played its part during the hundred and thirty years of its existence, and the long list of the battle honours of the Gordon Highlanders is eloquent testimony of the fighting qualities that they have ever shown. The Bavarians will not forget for many a year the day when, in the present war, they met the Gordons in the Zwartelen woods ; and the musketry of the 2nd battalion at Kruiseik will ever be a glorious memory.

Their bonnet badge is a stag's head front-faced, the neck rising out of a ducal coronet, which is the crest of the noble Scottish house of Gordon, with the word " Bydand " on a scroll below, the device being completed by a wreath of ivy, the badge of the Gordon clan.

THE QUEEN'S OWN CAMERON HIGHLANDERS

were raised as the 79th Foot by Cameron of Eracht in 1793, almost all the first strength of the regiment being of the Cameron name and kin. Until the South African War the regiment consisted of one battalion only, which has amassed a long list of honours, from " Egmont-op-zee " to " South Africa ; " and the story of the first months of the present war will not be complete without mention of the Cameron Highlanders' great work, as, for instance, at Troyon, at Kruiseik, and in the defeat of the Prussian Guard before Ypres. There were left of them on 12th November, 1914, only three officers and 140 men.

As the " Queen's Own," a title which they have borne since 1873, the Camerons have the blue facings of a royal regiment.

The regimental badge is a crowned thistle. That worn upon the bonnet is a figure of St. Andrew with his cross inside a wreath of thistles, which is charged with a ribbon inscribed " Cameron."

THE ROYAL IRISH RIFLES

are formed from the 83rd (County of Dublin) and the 86th (Royal County Down), both raised in 1793. The former, known at first as " Fitch's Grenadiers," in jocular reference to the small stature of the men, claims a long list of Peninsular honours with Picton's Division. The 86th, first raised as " Cuyler's Shropshire Volunteers," received their Irish title in 1812, and their nickname, the " Irish giants," from their fine physique.

The cap badge is the Irish harp, crowned, with the motto " *Quis separabit* " on a ribbon below. As in the case of all rifle regiments, there is no collar badge.

PRINCESS VICTORIA'S (ROYAL IRISH FUSILIERS)

Both battalions of this regiment were raised in 1793, the 1st being the 87th (Royal Irish Fusiliers) and the 2nd the old 89th (Princess Victoria's), and share a splendid record. The " Faugh-a-Ballagh " boys soon made their war-cry famous, as their nicknames " the old Fogs," and " the Aiglers " or " Eagle Takers," testify, and the 2nd battalion, " Blayney's Bloodhounds," do not lag behind. The 87th, at Barrosa, captured the first eagle taken in the Peninsular War, and for this exploit of Sergeant Masterson the regiment bears an eagle on the ball of the grenade which is its first collar badge.

The second collar badge is the coronet of the Princess Victoria.

For their cap badge the Royal Irish Fusiliers wear a grenade which bears upon the ball an Irish harp with the Prince of Wales's feathers above it.

THE CONNAUGHT RANGERS

inherit the title of the 88th, raised in 1793, and are formed from that regiment and the 94th Foot. The two regiments fought side by side in many of the Peninsular battles whose names figure in their joint list of honours. Picton called the 88th " the greatest blackguards in the army," till Fuentes d'Onor, when their magnificent charge won the day, and on their return he greeted them with " Well done, brave 88th." Being challenged by some of the men, whether they were still " the greatest blackguards," he replied, " No, no; you are brave and gallant soldiers; this day has redeemed your character." The nickname of the 88th, " the Devil's Own," is another compliment attributed to Picton.

It was earlier Indian service which gave them the badge of an elephant, which is worn as the collar badge. The cap badge is the crowned harp, with the regimental title on a ribbon below.

The 94th, known as " the Garvies," was raised originally as a Highland regiment, and with five others (the 72nd, 74th, 75th, 90th and 91st) abandoned the kilt in 1824 owing to the fact that they were mainly recruited out of Scotland. The 94th, however, is alone in having become Irish, for the other numbers will be recognised as those of five famous Scottish regiments, three of which have returned to the kilt.

PRINCESS LOUISE'S (ARGYLL AND SUTHER-LAND HIGHLANDERS)

The old " Argyllshires," raised in 1776 as the 98th Highlanders, and renumbered as the 91st Highlanders in 1802, received the title of " Princess Louise's Argyllshires " in 1872, on the occasion of the marriage of her royal highness with the Marquess of Lorne. They were made the 1st battalion of the regiment in 1881, the 2nd being the old 93rd (Sutherland) Highlanders, who were formed in 1800 from " the Sutherland Fencibles," raised by Elizabeth, Countess of Sutherland, in 1779.

A lengthy roll of battle honours shows that both battalions have rendered service to the Empire in Africa and India. The 1st covered itself with glory in the Peninsula ; the 2nd was " the thin red line " which at Balaclava bore unsupported the onset of the Russian horse, and routed them ; for which fine performance the Argyll and Sutherlands, alone among infantry regiments, carry the honour, " Balaclava," on their colour.

The bonnet badge consists of two L's reversed and interlaced, between the boar's head of Campbell and the cat of Sutherland, all surmounted by a coronet of the princess, and placed inside a circular band inscribed " Argyll and Sutherland," the whole being surrounded by a wreath of thistles. The collar badge shows a boar's head in a wreath of wild myrtle linked with a wreath of butcher's broom enclosing a cat-a-mountain [1] with the label from the arms of Princess Louise over all.

[1] The boar's head is the crest cf the Campbells, Dukes of Argyll. Wild myrtle is the badge of the clan. A wild cat is the crest of the noble Scottish house of Sutherland. Butcher's broom is the badge of the clan.

THE PRINCE OF WALES'S LEINSTER REGIMENT (ROYAL CANADIANS)

are the old 100th Foot combined with the 109th. Neither originated in the British Isles, the 100th having been raised in Canada in 1858 as a corps of volunteers for service in India, and the 109th (Bombay Infantry) Regiment was raised at Poonah in 1853, from which fact it derives its nickname of the " Poonah Pets." The Irish title dates from 1881. Till then the 100th had been known as the Prince of Wales's Royal Canadians.

The now familiar maple-leaf is one of the colour-badges of the regiment, and at one time the colours were wreathed with maple on Dominion Day. The 100th was the last British infantry regiment to be quartered in Canada.

The regimental number of the Canadians has given rise to the nicknames " the Centipedes," as well as " the Old Hundredth ; " " the Crusaders " is an allusion to their origin in a desire for far Eastern service, while " the Wild Indians," " Colonials," and " Maple Leaves " are self-explanatory.

The 109th have the curious nickname of " Brass-heads," which they earned by their immunity from sunstroke in India ; they were also called " the German Legion " from the number of Germans in their ranks in John Company days.

The badge of the Leinsters is the Prince of Wales's plume with a ribbon inscribed " The Leinster."

THE ROYAL MUNSTER FUSILIERS

are made up of the 101st (Royal Bengal Fusiliers) and 104th (Bengal Fusiliers), which, both being Indian regiments, take precedence only from their enrolment in the British establishment. Yet the 101st can trace its origin to a guard of honour to the East India Company, raised in 1652. It was re-embodied under Clive in 1756, and has a magnificent roll of honours won in India, beginning with the epoch-making field of Plassey and culminating at Delhi and the relief of Lucknow. It never saw England until 1868. The 104th has also a fine record of Indian and Burmese service. Up to the present the only honour earned outside Asia and shown on the colour of the Munsters is " South Africa, 1899–1902."

The 2nd battalion Munster Fusiliers formed part of the 1st Brigade in the original Expeditionary Force in 1914. Misfortune overtook them at Bergues in the retreat from Le Cateau on August 27th, and only 150 escaped capture with the help of the 15th Hussars.

The nickname of " the Dirty Shirts " is prized by the regiment as a reminder of the splendid work of the 101st at Delhi, where they fought in their shirt-sleeves.

The badge of the regiment is a grenade with a tiger and ribbon inscribed " The Munster," on the ball.

THE ROYAL DUBLIN FUSILIERS

are made up of the 102nd (Royal Madras) Fusiliers, and the 103rd (Royal Bombay) Fusiliers. These again are old East India Company regiments, the 102nd having been raised in 1748 as the Madras European Regiment from independent companies, some of which dated from the time of Charles I., and the 103rd having an unbroken record from its foundation in 1661. Thus, though the last regiment but one of the British Line, it has very nearly the longest history. Like the Munsters, all its many honours were derived from the East till the South African War, where it lost heavily and earned great distinction

The nicknames, the " Lambs " (102nd) and the " Old Toughs " (103rd), may refer to the tiger and elephant badges respectively. Both of these are borne, the elephant above the tiger, on the grenade which is the badge of the regiment.

THE RIFLE BRIGADE
(THE PRINCE CONSORT'S OWN)

was raised in 1800, a 2nd battalion in 1805, a 3rd in 1855, and a 4th in 1857. The regiment has earned 33 honours in a century, beginning as marines at Copenhagen on Nelson's flagship, including nearly all the Peninsular victories, Waterloo, the Crimea (where it won seven V.C.'s) and the Mutiny. It took part in both the defence and the relief of Ladysmith. William IV. told the Rifle Brigade, " Wherever there has been fighting there you have been, and wherever you have been you have distinguished yourselves."

The nicknames, " the Sweeps " and " the Greenjackets," both refer to the uniform, which is dark green with black facings.

The cap badge is a silver Maltese cross within a laurel wreath and surmounted by a crown and the honour " Waterloo." On the cross is a circle inscribed " Rifle Brigade " and enclosing a bugle. The honours of the regiment are inscribed on the cross itself and on a ribbon twined about the wreath.

THE ARMY SERVICE CORPS

was established in 1794, though it had been preceded in the 17th century by various transport corps raised for special purposes. It has had many changes of form and name, such as " Land Transport Corps," " Military Train," and " Commissariat and Transport Corps," and has had many abusive nicknames bestowed upon it, mostly in the form of perversion of its initials—as, " London Thieving Corps," " Murdering Thieves," " Moke Train," and the like. It has done sterling service where glory is not won, and honours are not added to its name. In the present war the corps has reached a degree of efficiency unimaginable save by those who have lived by its ministrations.

The badge is a crowned star charged with the garter within a laurel wreath, enclosing the monogram " A.S.C."

ROYAL ARMY MEDICAL CORPS

organised in its present form in 1873, has for its badge the
serpent and staff of Aesculapius, the god of healing and medi-
cine in Greek and Roman mythology. A laurel wreath and
the significant motto " *In arduis fidelis* " tell of the
devotion and the noble services of this distinguished corps,
while the crown which completes the design refers to its
royal title.

ARMY VETERINARY CORPS

founded in 1796, was re-organised and re-constituted on something approaching its present basis in 1881: but it was not until the South African War that rank and file were added to the officers, bringing the corps into its present fully developed form.

The 11th Light Dragoons in 1796 were the first to have a veterinary surgeon attached.

The nicknames " the Vets " and " Horse Doctors " need no comment.

The badge is a crowned laurel wreath enclosing the monogram of this hardworking corps.

ARMY CHAPLAINS' DEPARTMENT

was organised in its present form in 1858. It is under the command of the Chaplain-General, who ranks as a major-general, and consists of four classes of Chaplains to the Forces with the relative rank respectively of colonels, lieutenant-colonels, majors, and captains. The Chaplains of the permanent establishment are Church of England, Presbyterian, and Roman Catholic ; Acting Army Chaplains include also Wesleyans, Baptists, and Congregationalists.

The cap badge is a plain cross formy of black metal, ensigned with a crown, which device is also worn on the collar of the tunic. Chaplains wear on their black-edged shoulder-straps the badges of their relative rank.

ARMY ORDNANCE DEPARTMENT

traces its ancestry back to the early 15th century, one John Louth having been appointed "Clerk to the Ordnance" in 1418. The Ordnance Department was established in the Tower of London from 1455 to the middle of the 19th century, when it was moved to Woolwich. It handles all manner of stores, from shirts to shells, in the field.

Its nickname, "the Sugar-stick Brigade," refers to the red-and-white pattern of the braid of its uniform.

The badge is the only true coat-of-arms belonging exclusively to a corps. On the shield are three cannons, and on a chief (the upper part of the shield) three cannon-balls.

ARMY PAY DEPARTMENT

with which is associated the Army Pay Corps, was organised
in 1878 to take over the accountancy of the Army, till then
a regimental matter. The badge worn by non-commissioned
ranks is the script monogram A.P.C. ensigned with the royal
crown; officers wear the King's crest as their cap badge.

Although battle honours cannot fall to the lot of this
hard-working corps, the whole service is indebted to it for
its quiet and unseen labours. Its nicknames, " the Quill-
Drivers " and " Ink-Slingers," are not monuments of human
gratitude.

CORPS OF MILITARY POLICE

until 1880 consisting of men detailed for this duty from the
individual battalions, or, in war-time, detached for service
under the Provost-Marshal, are now a separate body, both
mounted and foot. The distinctive red covering of their caps,
worn in war-time with the khaki, as well as in peace with the
blue uniform, gives them their nickname of " the Redcaps."
The badge is the crowned royal cipher in a wreath.

ROYAL MARINES

By land and sea, as their motto declares, the Royal Marines have ever rendered magnificent service. Though founded in 1644, by an order in council, with a strength of 1200, they do not appear to have been continuously employed until about 1710 ; and for another century foot regiments frequently served as marines in naval operations, as the battle honours of several regiments testify. " His Majesty's Jollies, soldiers and sailor too," can turn their hand to any kind of fighting afloat or ashore, and their one honour, "Gibraltar," though typical enough of the amphibious nature of their service, gives no clue to their world-wide and ever honourable record. In this they uphold the tradition of " the Silent Service " to which they properly belong.

Their badge is the terrestrial globe encircled by a laurel wreath, and surmounted by a crown. Below it is the motto, " *Per mare per terram*," which so succinctly expresses the field of their activities and the scope of their history.

Lightning Source UK Ltd.
Milton Keynes UK
UKHW050022110121
376635UK00008B/101